The Poisoned Embrace

Ania Malina
Paris Dreambook
The Angelic Game

The Poisoned Embrace

A Brief History of Sexual Pessimism

Lawrence Osborne

PANTHEON BOOKS
NEW YORK

All rights reserved under International and Pan-American
Copyright Conventions. Published in the United States by
Pantheon Books, a division of Random House, Inc., New York.
Originally published in Great Britain by Bloomsbury
Publishing Ltd., London.

Translations are indicated in the bibliography; those
from the texts of Lamartine, Abel Barbin's autobiography,
Thénot, Barthélemy and Lacombe's *Don Juan* are my own,
for which I accept all responsibility.

I would like to thank Jim Holman in California for his
generosity and patience, and Gregor von Rezzori for illuminating
comments on the Jewish question.

Library of Congress Cataloging-in-Publication Data

Osborne, Lawrence, 1958–
The poisoned embrace : a brief history of sexual pessimism /
Lawrence Osborne.
p.   cm.
Includes bibliographical references.
ISBN 0-679-42723-6
1. Sex—Religious aspects—Christianity—History of doctrines.
I. Title: Sexual pessimism.
BT708.O73   1993   93-17326
233′ .5—dc20   CIP

Title-page illustration by Roberto de Vicq de Cumptich

Manufactured in the United States of America
First American Edition
9 8 7 6 5 4 3 2 1

Contents

Increase and multiply, and know that the cause of death is love

    Poimandres, Corpus Hermeticum, Tractate I

Introduction

There is a story, popular among modern writers, which concerns an old woman on a provincial Italian bus. Although there are occasional variations, the gist of the story is as follows: an old woman gets on to the bus as the writer is travelling between two small towns. Half crazed, and yet seemingly deliriously happy, she points to between her legs and shouts, *La bestia è morta!* – 'The Beast is dead!' At this point the young writer is reminded of certain philosophical truths. Namely, that this buried organ is a source of terror; and also that the Beast is only short-lived. In addition, he cannot help feeling a marked admiration for the strength of character of the crone who has realized that she is not decayed, hideous or beyond love but free. In his version of this anecdote, which seems to translate a common experience of young writers travelling on Italian buses, Czesław Miłosz notes: 'Both regret and triumph sounded in her voice – the triumph of liberation from the *beast of sex*.'

For Miłosz, the old woman, and probably all the embarrassed travellers in that bus, the *bestia* is a curse which has been tagged slyly on to the human form in order to divert it from more angelic persuasions. It is a shackle, more or less as eighteen centuries of Catholic theology have described it. Indeed, for the Early Fathers like Jerome and Ambrose it was not just the organ which could be described as bestial, but the instinct behind it as well. The instinct, like the anatomy, was man's short cut to death.

Sexual pessimism, as this theological equation of sexual love and death is known, may well be Catholicism's most eccentric trait. But for at least two hundred years now the aversion of the Early Fathers for sexual appetites and the human body (and their compensatory admiration for virgins and chastity) has been seen as the result of a force which has little to do with Christianity: the pessimistic cosmology of Gnosticism.

The first to air this view was Heine, in his book on religion in Germany, and it has been a constant theme of iconoclast theologians ever since. The most recent of these has been Uta Ranke-Heinemann,* who was recently expelled from the Church for insisting that this long history of what has come to be known as 'sexual pessimism' is not Christian at all, but has far older roots.

* For this and other references to contemporary texts, see the Bibliography at the end of the book.

Ranke-Heinemann, like Heine, points out that the New Testaments themselves, the core of Christian teaching, contain no passages of explicit sexual pessimism. Nor, contrary to popular myth, does the peculiar ferocity of later Christian thought find its roots in the Old Testament. Nor can it be said that the Classical world which Christianity replaced was a hot-bed of sexual licence: it was a platitude of both Greek medicine and Stoic moralism that the healthy controlled and suppressed their instincts. What is different about later Catholic theology is that sexual love is fully equated with death. And this equation comes fairly and squarely from Gnosticism.

Sexual pessimism, then, is the equation of sexual love outside the prerequisites of reproduction with death. Why should this equation have occurred in Christian thought and seemingly nowhere else? In what way did it create a history all of its own, with its own nightmares and monuments? In this book, I will trace this history through eight of these distinct nightmares: the Virgin, the Witch, the Leper, the Noble Savage, the Jew, the Oriental, the Androgyne and Don Juan. Eight may seem too unmagical a number for any foray into mystic thought (for the theology of sexual pessimism is just that), but the number could theoretically be extended almost indefinitely. I have chosen these eight simply for their familiarity and their accessibility. And I have begun, as Christians do, with the Garden of Eden, for it was the events in the Garden – indeed, the very nature of that Garden itself – which determined everything that followed. The Paradise of the Christian, unlike the revels in store for the Jew or the Muslim, is nothing more nor less than a celestial replica of Eden, the sublime state of sexlessness to which the virtuous dead return.

As this history seems to unfold, what is striking is that it was always shaped by a profound nostalgia for the innocence of Eden. We are the most fraudulent and inveterate of nostalgics, always mourning the loss of that unknown and vaguely Mesopotamian Garden. This nostalgia is inseparable from our pessimism, sexual and otherwise. And the expulsion, far from opening up untold possibilities – limitless reproduction, the wonders of agriculture and cities – only burdens us with a peculiar longing to be elsewhere, to be alive in a timeless past. It is in the context of this longing that sexual pessimism flourished.

Lastly, I have suggested that sexual pessimism, emerging into a rational age hostile to it, has transformed itself into an equally strange sexual optimism. From the belief that sex was the source of death, we have passed to the equivalent belief that it is the only source of life: from Augustine, to Wilhelm Reich. Yet the two attitudes are fundamentally the same. As Denis de Rougemont has shown, our sense of overwhelming sexual passion, a passion which is endlessly glorified and which now gives life its paramount value, derives from the Troubadours and Northern Mystics of the Middle Ages, and through them (how completely the wheel turns) from the secret tradition of Gnosticism itself. Nor can the Passion of the Cross be overlooked. Since *passio* referred to a disease, a suffering, we have ended up with a vision of love as a sublime act of crucifixion, and at the same time a mysterious source of therapeutic energy. This contradiction finds its fullest flowering as much in the present day as in the thirteenth century. Sexual pessimism may have been buried, at least partially, but it continues to nourish the grass that grows on its grave. It may even be that it has before it the possibility of a glorious resurrection, and the invention of other, even more ingenious, nightmares.

1

The Garden of Eden

'The Earthly Paradise' of Jan Brueghel hangs in
the Galleria Doria in Rome. From a distance,
its profusion of animals, of peacocks, swans and
foxes, all of them paired off as in Noah's Ark,
seems as ordered and tame as the private zoo of
some corrupt Renaissance pope. This is not nature,
after all, but a discreet arrangement of it. Even the
slanting bough on which the bearded macaque is
sitting with its mate and from which the golden
robe of a peacock hangs seems to have been laid
there on purpose, at a quaint angle over the duck
pond. Indeed, on the edge of that very same pond
a distinctly domestic-looking hound is prowling
through the reeds looking for an inattentive drake.
Nor does the inclusion of big cats, ibex and giraffes
convince you at all. This is not the primeval forest
according to Linnaeus; it is nothing but Eden pure
and simple. And if you wanted any proof of it, you
could strain your eyes towards a small clearing in
the middle distance and catch sight of two naked

bipedal wretches arguing over something dangling from a tree.

At first, you are not likely to be interested in them. Why, after all, look at a couple of pale humans when you can feast your eyes on crimson parakeets, white mares and a dazzling variety of bird life? But then, if this really is Eden, you are dimly aware that what is going on under that tree, however nonchalant the painter seems to be towards it, is actually *important*. It's a shame it's such a long way off, but even so you can still make out a long, thin, straggling thing unravelling itself from the tree towards the woman, who is carelessly reaching up towards it. With an uneasy shock of recognition you realize it is a snake. And, yes, the tree is a huge apple tree. And yes, the man seems to be pleading with her. He is almost beseeching her, holding up his hands in an attitude of prayer while a little greyhound stares up at him in alarm. What is it she has in her outstretched hand? Something for the snake to eat? Or an offering?

To be sure, they are not the only ones squabbling. Look at the lions. The male is stalking round the female baring his teeth, as if they are about to start savaging each other in earnest. And a couple of delicate wild cats are up hunting in the trees – do they kill things in Eden? All in all the animals seem perfectly indifferent to the funny hairless apes fooling about under the apple trees. Why should they worry? Up to now, they haven't been molested. And why should they care if the hairless female eats the apple or not? What difference will it make to Eden?

No one seems to be sure what exactly will happen when Eve starts munching that apple. Will the animals discover the pleasures of carnivorousness and begin slaughtering each other? And at what time will God stroll into the picture with his parasol and pruning shears, a plump head gardener looking for his favourite creation? We know that it will be late afternoon, and we can almost imagine which of the voluminous bushes the suddenly ashamed and nude original man is going to hide behind. But we cannot actually picture the change that will come about. The trees will still be there, overflowing with blossoms. The swans will still be sailing around between the lilies, and the stags will still be nosing about in the distant long grass. Nature is eternal, and so is the Garden. But the apes will no longer be there. The change in everything will be literally invisible, for it will have taken place within them. They will be howling somewhere on the outside, in the desert perhaps, in the blue mountains visible in the distance. Adam will be ploughing fields, cursing his bad luck. And Eve? She will have taken to the maternity ward.

The loss of this Garden might seem a mixed blessing. Certainly, it would be a beautiful place to take a picnic. But to spend years there, decades, centuries . . . *eternity*? Secretly, looking at 'The Earthly Paradise' in the Galleria Doria, we are glad that we escaped. For it is impossible to suppress the feeling that, contrary to all reason and in troubling defiance of everything you have learnt to associate with biblical lies, long, long ago, *we have been there before*.

The Garden of Eden is our first myth, and from the beginning the prophets wouldn't give up eulogizing a place they had never seen. Ezekiel described a mountain paradise bursting with flowers; Athanasius of Alexandria painted a Paradise in the image of India; and Moses bar Cephus, Bishop of Mosul in the ninth century, described a glittering wilderness through which a majestic river flowed, disobeying the laws of gravity and watering a wondrous plateau.

The cultivated intellectuals of the late Roman Empire created their own idylls in their visions of Eden. St Basil (AD *c.* 330–79) in his *Hexameron* created a lyrical panorama which encompassed the entire organism of the natural world. It described with sweeping grandeur the creation of natural harbours, the tropism of plants and the sex of trees. And as the saint repeatedly reminds his flock, in that blissful, long-gone world, the rose was without the thorn. What is curious about the dream of Eden is that it was always highly literal. The cartographers of the Middle Ages and later tried again and again to place it on the map. In one seventeenth-century map of the Middle East there is clearly visible a territory marked 'Eden' straddling the river Tigris between Babylon and the Persian Gulf. One can even imagine it with border posts and immigration controls. In the Sumerian myths, on the other hand, it was located in the Garden of Dilmun, also on the Persian Gulf, while in other topographies, notably that of Genesis, it was located to the north of Babylon, in the mountains of southern Armenia.

The physical location of Eden was of great importance, for if history began there through an actual transgression it was difficult to consign it to some vague, celestial sphere hanging in the ether. It had physically to exist. On the other hand, what happened there was more enigmatic than tradition confessed. Did Eve really come sprouting out of Adam's side in the form of an animate intercostal? Did sex actually occur in the Garden? And, most subtle and fiendish of all: how was Adam to have multiplied?

The Graeco-Roman intelligentsia which created the Catholic Church was in two minds. Philo of Alexandria for one shook his head disbelievingly over the tale of the rib. 'For how,' he said, 'could anyone believe that a woman, or a human being at all, came into existence out of a man's side?' There was then the problem of Adam's body. Did the Edenic man defecate or pass urine? Many denied it. Many also denied that Adam ever touched Eve carnally. But if that was the case, as Augustine was forced to put the question to himself, and if Adam before the Fall was sexless, incapable of the sin of procreation, how was he to have multiplied?

The problem had already been perceived in the

fourth century by Gregory of Nyssa in his *On the Making of Man*. Gregory was perplexed. He had noted that the angels had managed to procreate, for there were evidently countless thousands of them. Equally evidently, however, the angels did not have any genital organs, and so they must have multiplied asexually, somewhat like aphids. How had they done this? The answer was perfectly scientific, and even avant-garde for its time: by spontaneous fission.

Gregory is coy about angelic fission. He says, not surprisingly, that it is 'unspeakable and inconceivable to human conjectures, except that it assuredly exists'. Augustine asked how unfallen man would have done it: '. . . the male semen,' he concluded a little shakily, 'could have been introduced into the womb of the wife with the integrity of the female organ being preserved'. Is it necessary to say that we are not told how this miraculous form of frictionless coitus was actually to have been performed?

We cannot doubt, though, that these civilized alternatives to ejaculation were entirely possible. Adam could, if he had wanted, have chosen the path of the aphid or the earthworm, but for some inexplicable reason he opted for carnal love.

Gregory, needing to explain the existence of sex in the Garden, tells us that the Deity had foreseen man's craving to consort with animals, and particularly the one called woman. He had there-fore thoughtfully provided him with the necessary equipment. The Fall was not inevitable – otherwise why describe the angelic mode of reproduction as a possibility for Adam? But it was certainly foresee-able. And being foreseeable, the necessary genital arrangements could be made well in advance.

It is for this reason that we find in ourselves, 'instead of an angelic mystery of nature, that animal and irrational mode by which they now succeed each other'. But the source of this eerie nostalgia for hermaphroditic operations, as well as the ludicrous account of the genesis of anatomy, are not as Christian as they have come to seem. Somewhere between the Old and New Testaments and the Early Fathers a strange anxiety entered the picture. It was an anxiety Brueghel, for one, was intimately familiar with: the anxiety of being descended from that terrible, sinister couple under the tree.

What marked this couple out if not the fact that, quite suddenly and unlike any other animal, they had to cover up their bodies? Are their bodies not the worst thing about them? How ignoble they look next to the orlotans, the cranes and the shadowed elks. Their flesh is white, feeble . . . *disgusting*. They seem to be smothered by it . . .

The Fathers shared this disgust. But this revul-sion was not Christian in origin. For where is hatred of these miserable bodies mentioned in the Testa-ments? Their hatred, their sexual pessimism, came from elsewhere. The ancient world, strange to say, insisted that it came from the same geographical area as the Garden itself: from a cult which legend says was born in the Fertile Crescent. The cult was Gnosticism, and for its followers even the Garden itself was nothing but a sewer posing as a dream, a dream, moreover, induced in the mind of Adam and Eve by a peculiar and unfamiliar devil, a Satan named Ialdoboath.

What exactly was Gnosticism? This dangerous and pessimistic quasi-religion, armed with a violent cosmology which preached the metaphysical evil of matter, appeared on the fringes of the Graeco-Roman East just before the time of Christ. No one knows precisely from where it came, but a fragment of Greek writing on a fresco of Bishop Epiphanius at Faras Cathedral in Nubia refers darkly to 'that devilish wickedness from the land of the Persians'.

Gnosticism was not a church; it was a set of loosely interpreted cosmological principles. The principal of these, and the root of what theologians call its 'acosmism', is the blasphemous assertion that the universe was not created by God but by a group of skilful demons called the Archons, or Rulers. The Archons control the celestial spheres, and since the true God sits somewhat forlornly on the far side of a dazzlingly complex celestial machinery, he is hopelessly remote from the created world. In the more mystical Gnostic texts, such as the Apocryphon of St John, this Deity is all but unknowable. He is called 'Light without measure'.

The doctrine of the Alien God underlay all the

myriad eccentric Gnostic sects, and made the universe ungovernably nihilistic, as if the organization of Jehovah had suddenly retreated to the moon and decided to stay there. To the Christians, it was an intolerable denigration of Nature, for the only thing that the Gnostic believed in was his *pneuma*, or 'divine inner spark', which longed for the God which had created it and which could be made to disobey the Archons by a rebellion known as 'gnosis', or enlightenment.

For Gregory or St Basil the universe was an ordered, ingenious and pleasant place, reminiscent of an Arthur C. Clarke biosphere. But for the Gnostics it was a dungeon, a waxworks nightmare presided over by their Satan Ialdoboath, captain of the Archons. These latter created their own law, the *heirarmene*, or Universal Fate, which trapped the soul in what was usually referred to as the Noise of the World. While he was sitting in a prison in India, Judas Thomas, a Gnostic saint of the Apocrypha, sang to his friends the Gnostic 'Song of the Pearl' of this Noise of the World, putting into a lyric the yearning for an escape from its cacophony, and from the treacherous body which listened to it.

The German scholar Hans Jonas has shown how Gnosticism arose as a result of the fusion of three traditions: Hellenism, the margins of Judaism, and Persian Zoroastrianism. These three incongruous bedfellows came together in the Greek empire of Alexander in the fourth century BC, spawning a host of semi-magical cults. Hellenism provided the frame and much of the language. Judaism provided the mythological garb and the monotheism. And from the Persian root came Gnosticism's extreme dualism, its eschatological judgement and its pessimistic fatalism.

What had happened in the hybrid Greek cities of the Asiatic Empire was that Hellenism had metamorphosed into an oriental religion, with infusions of Babylonian magic and astrology and a doctrine of transcendence and salvation. And from Indo-Persian religion its cults derived their division of body and soul where the latter enters a heavenly realm of light after death.

From the East, then, came Gnosticism's demand that man should 'no longer come into being'. But as the oriental cults of the Hellenic Empire began to filter into Jerusalem, they came up against another force – what Kurt Rudolph called the 'critical self-dissolution at the fringes of Judaism'.

In the Jewish books, we do find many passages warning off the holy from the coil of flesh. In Ecclesiastes and in the Wisdom of Solomon we read: 'For the corruptible body presseth down the soul, and the earthy tabernacle weigheth down the mind that museth upon many things' (Wisd. 9:15); and '. . . blessed is the eunuch, which with his hands hath wrought no iniquity, nor imagined wicked things against God: for unto him shall be given the special gift of faith . . .' (Wisd. 3:14).

The Dead Sea Scrolls and the Gnostic Nag-Hammadi texts, discovered in 1945 in a cave in Egypt, bear many similarities to each other. Like the Gnostics, the Jewish fringe sects were practising ascetic withdrawal from the world, and had entered into a secret revolt against their horned law-giver and his bossy and totalitarian God. But Gnosticism's vituperation of Nature and all its urges was even more ferocious. For whereas even the most ascetic Christian and Jew might long for a return to the primeval innocence and sexlessness of the Garden, the Gnostic looked with horror on Eden's bubbling brooks and majestic plane trees. He saw himself as alone in a giant prison made seductive by mankind's use of demonic narcotics. Where was the exit from this nightmare if not in a subversion of all the Old Testament myths which held it in place? What was Moses if not the fraudulent law-enforcer of a corrupt demonic state? And if all this river of lies began with the misrepresentation of the Garden of Eden, what was the free Gnostic mind to do but retell the myth of Eden?

Around the year AD 180 the Bishop of Lyons, Irenaeus, wrote a book called *Adversus haereses* directed at crushing the multitude of heresies which had penetrated to the heart of the Christian flock itself. The 'heresies' described with such venom by Irenaeus are Gnostic, and his venom was the result of fear. Two hundred years later, the young

Augustine would succumb to the attraction of this rival religion, a religion so supple and so amorphous that it was often possible to be Gnostic and Christian at the same time, as was the case with the theologian Marcion, Irenaeus' near-contemporary.

According to Irenaeus the first true Gnostic was Simon Magus, that coxcombish trickster who flits in and out of the biblical story in the company of a female friend. In the first story of Danilo Kiš's *The Encyclopedia of the Dead*, for example, we see him organizing a climbing trick with a flaxen rope, and re-attaching the severed head of a calf to its body.* Simon was the second Redeemer figure after Christ himself, according to the Gnostics, and after him came a line of obscure and heteroclite prophets, whose writings have disappeared. There was Menander, then Saturninus of Syria, then Basilides of Antioch and Valentinus in the first century AD. All of the sects founded by these world-haters were different, but all of them merged in one distinctive feeling: their sexual pessimism.

In the Corpus Hermeticum, dated to the second century AD and attributed to Hermes Trismegistus, the first text, called the *Poimandres*, or Shepherd of Men, contains the earliest statement of this

---

* After moralizing on the horrors of existence ('on the horror known by lepers, on the hideous metamorphoses of women's breasts'), he floats skywards, 'arms beating like fish gills', his hair and beard streaming in the wind.

Gnostic sexual pessimism: 'And although created male and female,' it says, 'because of his derivation from the bisexual Father and sleepless from the unsleeping one, he is nevertheless overcome by love and sleep.'

The *Poimandres* informs us, rather startlingly, that there were seven original men, 'bisexual and sublime'. They lived through a period of bliss before the advent of sexual reproduction. Then God broke the bonds holding everything happily together and 'all living things previously bisexual were parted, as was man; they became on the one hand male and on the other female'. And God instructs them: 'Increase and multiply . . . and know that the cause of death is love.'

To Hermes the invention of sex was a cosmic disaster, somewhat analogous to the invention of typhoid. Moreover, the text continues:

> . . . he who has loved the body, which comes from the deceit of love, remains wandering in the darkness, suffering in his senses the things of death . . . it is because the source of the individual body is that abhorrent darkness from which the moist nature comes and from which the body is produced in the sensible world, and by which death is nourished.

It is interesting to remember that *Poimandres* was translated by Ficino into Latin in 1463 and became one of the most influential philosophical tracts of the Renaissance. Tractate VII of the Hermetica, however, goes even further:

> . . . this bondage of corruption, this cloak of darkness, this living death, this sensate corpse, this tomb you carry around with you, this robber who lives in your house who by the things it loves hates you . . . Such is the hateful tunic with which you have clothed yourself; it holds you down in a stranglehold.

The Gnostics convinced themselves that they could be saved only by self-castration. Yet another Gnostic source, this time the Gospel of Mary contained in a Coptic manuscript found at Achmim in Egypt called the Codex Berolinensis, tells us – as if we were patients being lectured to by a stern doctor advising on the dangers of bubonic plague – that sexual sin 'is a suffering which has nothing like itself, which has arisen out of what is contrary to nature'.

The sexual obsessions of the Gnostics shocked even the severest of Christians. Chrysostom, that great pioneer of virginity, was astounded at the excesses of the 'encratics', or Gnostic ascetics. 'I would not go so far as to call the encratics virgins,' he says, 'for their excess of asceticism is based on the idea that matter is metaphysically evil because its creator is not the supreme god.' In other words, when God is removed from the world, hatred of everything in it is limitless. But what Chrysostom failed to admit was that he himself, like so many involved in the creation of the Catholic Church, bore the internal wound inflicted by this very same heresy.

This was the point at which the Garden began to be a problem. The Gnostics had shown how difficult it was to make the story work. In their folkish stories they loved to retell most of the Judaic tales sarcastically and subversively, and with the Garden they went to town. Let us look at one example.

There is an obscure Gnostic book called the Gospel of St John. This contains a complete rewriting of the Eden story, which goes more or less as follows. The Archon Ialdoboath decided one day to create the Garden and to put the thing called man which he had created in it. He made the Garden as pleasant as possible. For instance, he invented things like flowers and rainbows, and all in all made the place a 'delight', which is the meaning of the word 'Eden'. The purpose of all this stimulation of poor Adam's five senses was to turn him into an obedient moral robot who would forget his divine origins. Now, marital intercourse arose simply because the Archon slipped it into Adam's mind; but as it happened it was the Archon himself who made Eve pregnant and who is therefore the true father of the human race. We are, then, descended not from the first man at all, but from a horned demon who has presumably passed on to us a part of his genetic make-up – i.e. we are guilty of filthy lusts, demonic pleasure-loving and other smutty habits of the aberrant angels. At the end of this wonderful story of depravity, the snake suddenly appears, behaving far too philosophically for a serpent, and, far from leading the primeval couple into temptation, opportunely wakes them up to the reality of the Garden. In other words, the snake is the first Gnostic and his gift is abrupt enlightenment – giving another sense altogether to the 'knowledge' which the Christians talked of as proceeding from these serpentine wiles.

The more extreme Gnostic sects identified the snake, therefore, with the Messiah, and for this reason gave themselves fancy names. One was called the Ophists (from the Greek *ophis*, or 'serpent') and another the Nassenes (from the equivalent Hebrew word *nahas*). Adam sleeps, then, in the 'drunkenness of the world'; there is no Fall, for he is already fallen.

Neither Jews nor Christians recognized much in the rhetoric of these fanatics who called the body the 'grave'. The chilling idea of the living dead, however, quickly scored a sensational success. That the body is a kind of perambulant cadaver must be one of history's more cruel and successful tropes. And who knows what the root of this success might be? An ancient terror of the venereal diseases which we know the Roman Empire spread through its rapid urbanization? An exaggerated sense of the ritual uncleanliness which we see described in the famous account of gonorrhoea in Leviticus? We know only that, even after many centuries, it could insert itself into the gaze of an artist staring into the fertile depth of a tamed wood where, gesticulating under a tree, two naked apes argue over an apple. Is it this we see in the horrified and defensive gesticulations of the man, who obviously wants to keep his virginity for eternity? Or have we missed the point altogether? Is the painting in reality by an unrepentant nudist and nature lover who is secretly disapproving of the man's craven frigidity? If this were the case, we would be free to imagine Gnosis or ascesis as itself the snake, bending down to give Eve a slimy or fatal kiss. We could even imagine it as something smaller, almost invisible, a tiny creature such as a maggot or a worm. And as we indulge in this extravagant allegorizing, we can imagine that as this 'worm' crawled into the core of its chosen apple, it began to take on the ascetically radiant aspect of a *virgin*.

2
The Virgin

It has long been known that virgins are magical. In ancient Rome, the Vestal Virgin Tuccia once performed the incredible feat of carrying a sieve filled with water from the Tiber to her sanctuary, while another virgin, this time of supernatural strength, dragged a ship off a sandbar in the same river, something which – it had, reluctantly, to be admitted – only a virgin could do.

Nor is that the end of virgins' talents. Alone of all God's race, they have the power to tame the unruly unicorn. The most mysterious painting of a virgin is Domenichino's 'Girl with a Unicorn', part of the frescoes of the Farnese Palace in Rome executed in the first years of the seventeenth century when the artist was working there under Annibale Caracci. Of course, we have no idea if the girl in the green mantle and bare feet holding a frolicking white unicorn in her arms is actually a virgin, but given the reputation of the latter, what else could she be? Academics love to eulogize Domenichino's 'tender, melancholy style', which is sufficient reason to give him a wide berth; nor, on the whole, whatever these same academics say, is it easy to fall in love with the Renaissance Virgin with her surreal levitations, her multitudes of tonsured camp followers and her doe-eyed placidity. On the whole, Circes, Mary Magdalene, Antiopes or the plump denizens of Cerquozzi's Turkish baths are better able to monopolize the gaze than that maternal vessel whom Augustine called a 'sealed fountain'. Yet the adolescent holding the horned white pony with affection is not *the* virgin, but an ordinary one. She is enigmatic because unnamed. Not even the fantastic animal which she has befriended in that slightly gloomy landscape makes her incredible to the imagination. She is as humdrum and strange as that great domesticized virgin painted by the Master of Flémalle which hangs in the London National Gallery under the beguiling title of 'Madonna and Child before a Fire Screen'.

Why are these two paintings – the one an anonymous teenager fondling a unicorn, the other a matron sitting with her writhing charge in front of a fire screen – the most obscure and incomprehensible of virgins? It is because they are not mystical. The Master of Flémalle's Virgin lives in a comfortable early fifteenth-century merchant's house, not dissimilar to the glass-windowed and probably chimneyed bedroom of Van Eyck's Giovanni Arnolfini. Recent innovations in domestic ventilation and chimney flues have made it warmer, cosier and more comfortable than the stone halls of earlier paintings. There are foot rests for the reader, plenty of manuscripts lying about, and, of course, fire screens. Not a trace of donkey mangers, bits of straw or bearded orientals following stars. In fact, through the window we can see a busy industrial town, where the owner of the house (Joseph the carpenter?) trades in flax and wool, and perhaps does his carpentry for a weekend hobby. There is virtually no cumbersome iconography, no vaulted halls, no puffs of heavenly smoke or gilded nimbi. *And yet . . .* it is said that the Master painted only four pictures, all of which were at the abbey of Flémalle-le-Liège, a place which in fact never existed. Although the Master might have been Robert Campin, no one really knows who he was. He has left one of the few virgins whose anatomy is credible, whose long and slightly ungraceful fingers (puckering a nipple which the infant seems uninterested in) and staid, even ugly face are the marks of her miraculous feat – a feat whose gynaecological perversity suddenly seems plausible.

Just as we believe, looking at Domenichino's scene with all the recovered gullibility which we should never have lost, that virgins can tame unicorns, so looking at this Gothic merchant's wife, holding her child close to her breast, we believe – with a shock of embarrassment – that that other Mary, the dark-skinned Aramaic-speaking proletarian hiding out in the cowshed, could have given birth while her hymenal tissue remained inexplicably intact.

Today the irrationality of the Virgin myth is either a nuisance or a torment to us. Rather than believe that our own culture could have ingested such an incredible fantasy, we look to a textual conspiracy on the part of the Early Fathers or a botched translation of the Septuagint from Hebrew to Greek in the third century BC. It is more comforting to explain the Virgin away in these terms than to believe that Christianity in its entirety could have been tainted with such a childish and oafish ignorance of basic gynaecology.

Uta Ranke-Heinemann, the revisionist German theologian who has traced the roots of Christian virgin-worship and the cult of celibacy back to their pre-Christian Stoic and Gnostic roots, has put the case for wholesale revision as follows.

The virgin birth, such as we find it in Christian orthodoxy, was intended as a metaphor for messianic rejuvenation. It was understood as such in the first century AD and what has happened since is brutally simple. The Early Fathers distorted New Testament innuendo, glossed over evidence of Jesus's blood relations and created, for reasons of their own, a grotesque biological ethic in which the Virgin reigned supreme.

Then there is the matter of the Septuagint translation. The original Hebrew for the word 'virgin' has the word *alma* in the line from Isaiah 7:14: 'A virgin shall become pregnant and bear a son and call him Immanuel.' *Alma* does not necessarily mean virgin, but can equally mean 'young girl'. The Greek version, however, uses the word *parthenos* or 'virgin', and the myth of the Virgin bearing the saviour is set on its way.

As it happens, the word *parthenos* does not necessarily mean virgin either, and in fact is a good translation of the term 'young girl'. But the revisionist is in the right when it comes to the absence of virgins in any of the original New Testament texts – the only ones which mention a virgin birth are Luke 1 and Matthew 1, and they do so only through late additions. Mark is silent on the subject, and so is Paul. Parthenogenesis appears nowhere as a literal truth, and does not emerge as an immaculate Christian virtue founded upon a real event until the third century AD. And it is here that Ranke–Heinemann, like Heine, sees the invisible but potent hand of Gnosticism.

By the time Gregory of Nyssa wrote his *On Virginity* in the fourth century, he was able to express misgivings which were no longer purely Christian. 'The bodily creation of children,' he wrote, 'is more an embarking upon death than upon life for man.' But when Jerome in Homily 23 wrote that the widow (and, by implication, the virgin) 'who gives her life over to pleasure is dead while she is alive', he was speaking the language of Gnosis pure and simple.

In fact, the Virgin was Gnosticism's greatest

vehicle. By means of her, and the blessed but hopelessly impossible condition which she represented, Gnostic pathology was able to enter into the Christian mainstream by the back door, and so impose itself at the heart of Western sexuality. For in the hands of her acolytes the Virgin became, not metaphor or parable, but blind, irrational reality. Writers on Mariology are always stressing that literal readings of the Virgin birth are beside the point. The ingenious sophistries needed to keep Mary intact – hymenally speaking – not just before her childbirth, but after and during it as well, are repeatedly dismissed as irrelevant, despite the fact that denial of these amazing facts actually caused Jovinian to be scourged on the advice of Ambrose and Bonosus to be excommunicated. But the question of the biology of Mary is not, in any case, as irrelevant as it is sometimes made out to be.

In the Apocryphal Gospels (the First Gospel of James 19–20 and in the Pseudo-Matthew 13:3–5) we find the enigmatic figure of the suspicious Salome, who is present during the actual birth of Christ. On Christmas night, Salome is overwhelmed with curiosity and understandable scepticism, and so pushes her fingers into Mary's vagina. But what she finds there is not the free passage her commonsensical mind had been expecting, but the membranous barrier which signifies a miracle of unparalleled enormity.

The resistance which Salome's fingers encounter on Christmas night, however, is not merely a sign; it is the very thing which makes the miracle possible as miracle. Twentieth-century Christians may well be anxious to disburden themselves of the awkward questions arising from this event, but for theologians the intactness of Mary was not merely a manner of speaking. If Mary was not sealed like a jar, if she was not a 'sealed fountain', then Christian time would not begin with a miraculous revelation. Like Eden, the Virgin had to be real.

The tremendous charisma which the hymen had for Christians can be gauged from the entry on Virginity in D'Alembert's *Encyclopedia*. For when the intellectuals of the Enlightenment wanted to damage Catholicism at its most vulnerable point, they went straight for what they called the 'dogma' of the hymen. Written by the Chevalier de Jaucourt and summarizing the views of the physician Bouffon, the entry states categorically that the hymen does not exist, that it is a primitive fantasy invented by barbarous theologians to enslave the female sex:

It is this kind of madness which has made a real entity of the virginity of maidens. Virginity, which is a moral fact, a virtue which consists solely in the purity of the heart, has become a physical object with which all men are concerned. Upon this object they have established opinions, customs, ceremonies, superstitions and even judgements and punishments.

The Chevalier then states, with the breathless confidence of the enlightened liberal:

> Anatomy itself leaves the existence of the hymen totally in doubt, as well as the multiform carbuncles whose presence or absence has long been regarded as indicating the certainty of defloration or virginity. Anatomy, I say, permits us to reject these two signs not simply as inconclusive but as downright fantastic.

The Church wanted its metaphysics and ethics grounded in biology, whenever possible. It was unfortunate for women that it eventually chose the Aristotelian variety, for reasons which will become apparent, a peculiarity of which was that it did in fact contain no scientific account of the hymen. As Giulia Sissa has shown in an interesting book on Greek virginity, the hymen was totally absent from Greek medicine. Nowhere is it ever described, either by Galen or by the Hippocratics. The Romans, it is true, suspected its presence, as must have the people who wrote down the story of Salome, but their awareness of it was purely anecdotal. Throughout the Christian centuries, paradoxically, this crucial piece of female anatomy – cornerstone of an entire ethic – was indeed, for all intents and purposes, just what the Chevalier de Jaucourt described it as being: a dogma emanating from 'a kind of madness'.

*   *   *

We think of Christianity as a sort of broom sweeping down upon the corrupt and promiscuous pagan world and brushing it away with energetic strokes. Certainly, the Christians portrayed themselves as unique worshippers of virginity. Chrysostom, for one, had no doubt that the dirty Jews could never have loved virgins, any more than could the equally besmirched Romans. He wrote: 'The Jews disdained the beauty of virginity, which is not surprising, since they heaped ignominy upon Christ himself, who was born a virgin. The Greeks admired and revered the virgin but only the Church of God 'adored her with zeal' (*On Virginity*). Ambrose, that great champion of the chaste, could only agree: 'This virtue is, indeed, our exclusive possession . . . nowhere are there living creatures in which it occurs.'

What seemed to please these writers was the ability of virginity to set Christians apart, not just from other human beings, but from all other animals as well. Yet their claims are a little exaggerated, for all the major philosophies of late Antiquity boasted of their virginity and the Christians were merely trying to outdo them. The fusion of Greek and Gnostic conceptions of virginity in Christianity did, however, create a unique combustion, and with time the Christian virginity did indeed become 'exclusive'. Nevertheless, the venerable view that this new religion represented a major rupture with the pagan world is untrue. Foucault, in his essay on Cassian, even goes so far as to say that the coming of Christianity was 'barely noticeable' as far as the cult of chastity was concerned, and that to talk of a 'Judaeo-Christian' sexual ethic is virtually meaningless. The hybrid which emerged between the fourth and seventh centuries as the Catholic Church was the end result of a confused synthesis of all the warring strains of late Antiquity, and as far as the mystical condition of virginity was concerned Christianity did not merely add shame to the Greek virgin goddess Diana, as Marina Warner suggests – it went to the Greeks for its ideal of shame as well.

What was this shame? And in what way is it the ancestor of our own?

The Greeks were obsessed by the virgin's masks, by her ability to disguise herself. A woman might look and behave like a virgin, but her inner virginity was completely invisible, since Greek doctors did not recognize the hymen. Virginity, therefore, could be detected only by a supernatural ritual. And the virgin herself, possessing as she did an inner character which was invisible, was the vessel of a mystery.

These virgin-detecting tests were highly poetic. The writer Achilles Tatius recounts several of them from Asia Minor which leave no doubt as to their symbolic content. The would-be virgin was led to a river ghoulishly named Styx outside Ephesus, which was a kind of riparian lie-detector. The virgin swore that she was chaste and her words were then written down on a tablet and hung around her neck. When this had been done, she stepped into the river up to her calves. If she had lied, the water would rise, boiling and splashing, and cover the tablet. And in a second ordeal described by Tatius, from the same region, the virgin was led to a cave where a set of Pan's pipes were kept; if the girl was a genuine virgin the pipes started playing themselves. As Sissa says: 'Virginity is greeted with a sweet, divine melody.' Another writer, Aelian, described another virgin ordeal from the region of Lanuvium in Italy. Here the sacred virgins were made to climb blindfold down into a cave situated in the middle of a forest. In the cave they served cakes to a serpent. The omniscient reptile, seeing through their earthly disguises, was able to detect the true virgins from the false and would accept cakes only from the former. The cakes of the deflowered, on the other hand, were carried off by ants after being reduced to crumbs so that the forest should remain pure.

The seduced young girl in Greek society was treated with unmitigated harshness. According to Solon, writing in the sixth century BC, *phthora*, or seduction, was the only ground on which an Athenian citizen could be reduced to slavery. The racial continuity of the Athenian state was embodied in its national virgin, and the inviolability of her body had to be reflected in the actual bodies of her female citizens. It is worth recalling that the punishments for loss of virginity in sixth-century Athens were far more cruel than anything administered by the penitentials of Christian Europe. The very *diaphtheirein*, meaning 'to seduce', originally denoted a physical disintegration (it was also used for 'abortion'). Aristotle uses the term *phthora* to describe any process of dissolution in the natural world. The seduced virgin was stripped of everything that gave her her identity. She was unfit for marriage. She could be put up for sale by her own father. And even her child would have to bear the insulting description of *parthenios*, offspring of a seduced virgin, for the rest of his or her life.

Two things emerge from these curious facts. Firstly, that the West established its relation to the female body – both as nude and as virgin – in the Classical period of Antiquity. And secondly, that virginity for the Greeks was not limited to any period of a woman's life, but was associated with an intense, unmistakable attitude towards sexuality.

That sexuality, when it came to the undeflowered girl, was remorselessly and inexplicably pessimistic. Why was it that the famous Greek doctors failed to spot the hymen? It couldn't have been from lack of awareness of the female genitals, or from a lack of sensitivity to the issue of virginity. The word 'hymen' is, after all, a Greek word, and the wedding song in Classical Greece was known as a *hymenaois*. The nuptial procession, or *nymphagogia*, was accompanied by excited shouts of 'Hymen! Hymenaois!' Yet it remains a fact that the Greek conception of virginity was inexplicably divorced from observation. Perhaps they had an enviable talent for not seeing what they did not want to see? Perhaps they possessed an irreproachable genius for lying?

The 'hymen' itself was given a mythological etymology, relating it to the god Hymen who had the misfortune to die on his wedding night. What is actually referred to is uncertain. What was it that 'died'? Galen used the word to describe an all-encompassing membrane covering the body's internal organs. In his exhaustive *Anatomicae administrationes*, written between AD 169 and 195, he describes a delicate, protective envelope of tissue which the dissector must remove with great care in order to expose the organs beneath without damaging them. In his introduction to Book 18 of the *De usu partium*, Galen proudly states: 'There is nothing which I have not spoken of in detail.' But there was one exception. The vaginal portion of the hymen is not mentioned once.

Galen's failure to mention the hymen is surprising in the light of his thorough dissection of the vagina. He certainly knew the difference between, say, the labia and the clitoris, even if, like the hymen, the latter was not understood as an organ in its own right. Another famous Greek working in Rome well known for his gynaecological work was Soranus of Ephesus. Soranus wrote in his *Gynaikeia* that the female genitals bore the name *sinus*, or 'gulf', and that it was a 'hymen' which was 'nervous'. The vagina in its entirety, therefore, was a kind of membrane, a balloon of subtle tissue whose delicacy was an object of wonder.

Soranus then goes on to raise the question of the 'membrana virginalis', and his is the first text to do so. But the hymen is not taken seriously for a moment. Far from it. 'In virgins,' he writes:

> the vagina is depressed and narrower, because it contains ridges that are held down by vessels originating in the uterus; when defloration occurs these ridges unfold, causing pain: they burst (the vessels), resulting in the excretion of blood that ordinarily flows . . . In fact, the belief that a thin membrane grows in the middle of the vagina, and that it is this membrane which tears in defloration or when menstruation comes on too quickly, and that this same membrane, by persisting and becoming thicker, causes the malady known as 'imperforation', is an *error*.

Soranus' careful probing of numerous virgins had left him with no impression of this delicate barrier! It did leave him with enough information to describe all the pathologies unique to virgins, from imperforations to atresia and the membranous obstruction known as a *meninx* and needing to be removed by surgery. But nowhere in this sophisticated explanation of virginal characteristics is the hymen admitted. Fourteen centuries later the Parisian anatomist Ambroise Paré, working in the mid-sixteenth century, was similarly unable to find evidence of the hymen in the bodies of young girls retrieved from the morgue of the Hôtel-Dieu in Paris. 'Some anatomists,' he writes in a sure tone, 'have held that virgins have a membrane or panniculus in the cervix which is broken in the struggles of Venus. This is implausible for one finds no such panniculus in the anatomy of virgins.'

This delusion is one of the most extraordinary perversities of medical history. Did Paré not feel the hymen because he knew Galen had declared it wasn't there? Both Soranus and Paré, however, speak of the belief that it *was* there. The Romans at least had their suspicions and refused to give them up. And the first medical account of the hymen was written by a Roman, one Servius, in the fourth century. Nevertheless, even the Romans kept on imbuing the 'curtain', as they called it, with supernatural associations. The god Hymen was said to live in it, and to be the first victim of the wedding night – experiencing, one would think, one of the most horrible deaths imaginable. Augustine, in the *City of God*, sarcastically describes the young bride losing her virginity: the marital chamber is crammed with bustling deities waiting for the act. There is Father Subigus (the Subduer), Mother Prema (the Presser), Goddess Pertunda (the Puncturer) and of course wily Virginensis, who seems to be anxious to lose herself. And why is Goddess Puncturer there? What is being pierced if not the hymenal veil? '. . . what is the function of the Goddess Pertunda? She should blush for shame and take herself off! Let the bridegroom have something to do for himself! It would be most improper for anyone but the husband to do what her name implies.'

The countless doctors and midwives who exercised their entrepreneurial flair by offering a hymen-restorative service had no need to perform elaborate operations with a sewing needle. A perfumed pessary was simply inserted into the chamber to alter and revitalize its appearance. The victims of divine rape, however, did not have even this aromatic expedient. Since the classical Lothario of the celestial kind was able to enter and leave women's bodies without leaving the slightest trace (not even a drop of blood), it has to be assumed that at this period in her evolution the virgin was able to reseal herself by thaumaturgics. If, on the other hand, she was raped by a mere mortal, shame and the tumescence of pregnancy caused her inner defilement to extrude itself. The Church may have adopted the Roman suspicion of the veil covering the entrance of the vagina, but confusion over this tiny web of 'sinous' tissue was actually increased because the Church could not really get used to the idea of letting people introduce their fingers into the hushed and darkened room of the virgin's vagina. Augustine himself was shocked at the thought of prying midwives' fingers. And what if the examiner accidentally pushed her fingers through the precious veil? In the case of that horrific accident, would the virgin still be a virgin?

Augustine constantly used the word *integritas*. The virgin is a walled garden, a *hortus clausus* sealed with locks and bolts. 'This gate,' he booms, 'shall remain locked.' Like a bottle of rare port, she is stoppered with a *signaculum*, or seal. But like the Pythia, she nevertheless makes an offering of her body to her Lord, who penetrates her by means not disclosed to physics. And like that mysterious oracle, her body is a vessel through which a divine enigma flows. However much Classical scholars resist the comparison, there is something of the Greek oracle in the Virgin: both are devoid of personal ambition, both are sexless, both are cut off from any real social relations. While the Pythia received her inspirational vapour through her sexual organs, the Virgin could, at the right moment, be pierced by beams of sunlight. Hence both these two virgins, Christian and pagan, placed themselves, in Sissa's words, in 'an ideal state of reception'. And when their supernatural husbands arrived they opened, like hushed electronic doors, to let him in.

Virginity was so delicate a problem that it propelled the theological mind to new heights of theoretical brilliance. In his tract *On True Virginity* Basil of Caesarea founded the doctrine of the Immaculate Conception – an ingenious stroke which made Mary not only a virgin but a super-virgin, one untainted even at her own birth by the contaminating secretions of love. Basil based his contention on the sound observation that vultures can be impregnated by wind.

In this shrewd argument, the Caesarean was only following the empirical path of science. Had it not been proved that weasels could be impregnated through their ears? Origen gave his examples of natural parthenogenesis ... bees emerging from oxen, snakes from corpses and so on. That the Virgin should have received the fructifying celestial spermatazoa through her ear seemed only natural.

It was not the demonstrations of science, however, that had led Origen and Basil to devise an unprecedented virginity as the origin of Christian history. The craving for virginity came first, and it was a craving as strong as hunger. The Gnostics shrouded it with an orchidaceous mysticism. The Gnostic theologian Marcion calmly declared that Christ was not made of flesh at all but of a phantasmal material which Mary could have expelled without much difficulty, somewhat like giving birth to a gust of air. This Gnostic tradition of the insubstantiality of Jesus, however, gave rise to the old problem of defecation. How, like the phantomic Adam, was he supposed to have defecated? Valentinus indignantly insisted, nevertheless, that Jesus never habituated urinals or worse: being the son of a virgin and bodiless, 'he had so great a power of continence that the food was not corrupted in him, since he himself was not perishable' (Letter to Clement, iii: 59, 3). Could the son of a virgin, after all, have something so vulgar as a stomach? We are not told whether Mary was sometimes forced to evacuate herself, but it seems unlikely in the light of the imagery with which she was encrusted. A great effort was needed on the part of Christians to get Christ's body back, and Tertullian, as we have seen, eventually launched a vicious attack on Marcion, though he still did not disclose Jesus's defecatory habits. But if the Christians defended Christ's flesh against accusations of ghostliness, they were still seduced by the mystification of celibacy, and by the notion of the Virgin as a 'cloud', a piece of matter beyond comprehension. Dreaming of her, they were like children wondering to themselves if it is possible to sit, ride or cavort on clouds – or whether one falls straight through them to certain death.

For the Greeks, as for the Romans, virginity was a stage in a woman's life from which she departed at marriage, and to which she returned in old age. The latter was a thankful recuperation of her former virginity. For the Gnostics, however, marriage and reproduction themselves were nothing but a means to sell more souls into slavery. What excuse was there for either? Why bog down more souls in the toxic waste of matter?

The Greeks made virginity a social code as well as an enigma, but the Gnostics turned it into a kind of Holy Ghost. Their Mother Goddess, Prunicos-Sophia, was an incarnation of virginity, and her mystery was celebrated with mind-numbing obscurantism. In the Gnostic book known as *Barbelognosis*, she is described as 'the perfect

power . . . the aeon of glory . . . she became
the First Man, which is the virgin spirit, the
threefold male, the one with the three powers,
the three names, the three begettings, the aeon
which does not grow old, the bisexual . . .' And
so, while the Greek virgin had a very real sexual
drive which was definitely female, the Gnostic
virgin was self-contained. She was not really a
she at all, but a sexless human worm, able, in the
last resort, to impregnate herself. And that, in the
Gnostic book called the *Apocalypse of Adam*, is just
what she did.

The mystical conception of Mary as a cloud, or
a 'cloud of desire' as in the *Apocalypse of Adam*, is
found in the Early Fathers as well. In his eleventh
Homily, for example, Jerome interprets a line from
Isaiah, 'See, the Lord is riding on a swift cloud on
his way to Egypt', by recasting it as, 'Behold the
Lord has entered Egypt of this world on a swift
cloud, the Virgin.'

In the Gnostics, too, the Virgin becomes a vessel
through which fluids pass without touching her – as
if she were a kind of magical pipe made of a material
which never rusts. Describing the doctrines of the
Gnostic Valentinians, Epiphanius says: 'But they
say that his body was brought down from above,
and passed through the Virgin Mary like water
through a pipe, without having received anything
from the Virgin's womb, but he had a body from
above . . .' (*Panarion*, 31:7).

For Epiphanius, the Virgin was a kind of blissful

void. The Christians, on the other hand, wanted a real woman, one who could at least breast-feed. Her vagina was locked tight, it has to be admitted, and her cervix was sealed with mystic wax. But she was certainly sexed. Sexed, that is, as a breast-feeder. Yet in her plump smiles and demure, downward-looking glances, in her soft dimples and her feeling of ease in Tuscan landscapes, there is still a whiff of the desert. She is a Bedouin deep down, an austere nomad who has settled in a Sinai monastery and left only her ears open to the male sex. 'This is the flower of the ecclesiastical seed,' Cyprian declared in the third century AD, 'the grace and ornament of spiritual endowment.' What he was really praising was a mutated woman whose insides were more than a little troubling. The problem was quickly spotted by Tertullian in *On the Veiling of Virgins*, where he nervously asks if Mary was actually a woman or another kind of being altogether. Chapter VI of that work therefore has for its title 'The parallel case of Mary'. Did Paul in Galatians, he asks, suggest that the essence of virgins and women are utterly different? But in order to preserve the miracle of Mary's intact virginity, her femininity could not be put in doubt. She had to have ovaries, a womb and all the normal complicated tubes. She had to menstruate, even if this was against her pure nature. Her sex was the key to her achievement.

The Father twists and turns. In the end, he finally declares that virgins can be women, and vice versa!

Yet he is still left with the tormenting problem of the virgin's vulnerability. After all, if she is a woman, she must like doing what women do, and what women like doing is *losing* their virginity. This is a great problem for the natural order: they must be virgins, but they dislike being virgins. A certain amount of pressure, then, is needed. In chapter XV, sinisterly entitled 'Of fascination', he declares that the virgin is a menace even to herself:

> Nay, but true and absolute virginity fears nothing more than itself. Even female eyes it shrinks from encountering. Other eyes it has. It betakes itself for refuge to the veil of the head as to a helmet, as to a shield, to protect its glories against the blows of temptations, against the darts of scandals, against suspicions and whispers . . .

Unless this is a prophylaxis against what the monk thinks is the terrible power of lesbianism, it presents us with the strange and edifying spectacle of young girls looking forward lustfully to peeping at themselves in mirrors. Yet how can the virgin lust after her own virginal self? How can she contain the poison to stain her own gaze? All the Fathers agreed with Jerome when he declared that virginity was 'a sacrificial offering to Christ'. They saw the virgin as spoken for and watched over her with all the jealousy of a doting father misanthropically spying on a rebellious daughter.

With time, this grandiose surveillance began to suffer fatigue. In the Middle Ages doctors began to assert that, since women produced their own semen, they needed to expel it regularly, and if they didn't they became peculiar. Popular handbooks of female disorders such as the *De mulierium affectibus* claimed that the illness of hysteria was caused by an absence of healthy coitus. The West's first sexologist, the eleventh-century doctor Constantine the African, wrote extensively on the nefarious effects of virginity in his *Viaticum*. The mysterious affliction known as *suffocatio matricis*, or suffocation of the womb, wrote Constantine, came directly from wretched virginity: 'When the woman has no commerce with a man, the sperm accumulate and there is born from it a smoke which rises to the diaphragm, for the diaphragm and the womb are linked . . .'

But if the virgin was unhealthy, temperamental and filled with smoke, why did she not go away? Because she was too potent a symbol? 'Christ,' wrote Irenaeus, 'would not have been one truly possessing flesh and blood, by which He redeemed us, unless He had summed up in himself the ancient fornication of Adam.' He did this by being born between a woman's legs. And what was woman, after all, even a virgin, if not a clone of Eve, and so a mirror of death?

40

3

The Ordered Scheme

Today, medieval scholasticism is synonymous with the body-hating mentality of Christian sexual pessimism. And indeed, it was its greatest vehicle. During theology's golden age, between the twelfth and fourteenth centuries, that pessimism enjoyed its finest theoretical blossoming; not for nothing does Ranke-Heinemann dub this same golden age 'woman's darkest hour'. We see the high Middle Ages as the Dark Ages of sexual relations.

Yet the heart of this great system is a vision of love – a vision partially as ecstatic and intricate as that of Dante in the *Paradiso*, but also made unbearable by a sexual pessimism so exquisitely organized that at first its pathological folly seems almost endearing.

Consider its enormous vocabulary. How are the bodily contacts classified? Aquinas himself gives us the following list: 'filth' (*immunditia*); 'a stain' (*macula*); 'foulness' (*foetidas*); 'defilement' (*pollutio*);

41

'vileness' (*turpitudo*); 'disgrace' (*ignomina*), and so on. The Gnostic tone of scholastic thought hardly needs much emphasizing. If one wanted an example of its typical excesses, one could point, as eminent historians of contraception do, to the notorious marital embrace known as the *amplexus reservatus*, which was advocated by the thirteenth-century theologian Cardinal Huguccio. This 'restrained embrace' was a complicated affair, in which the man gave an orgasm to the woman but withdrew when she was satisfied without ejaculating himself, so preserving his virtue, though presumably not hers. One could easily say that only the tormented theological imagination could dream up so disciplined and so painful a finesse. And yet the *amplexus* was not merely practised by husband-ascetics anxious to enter Paradise, but also, for many centuries, by the aristocracy, as a considerate and elegant form of contraception. And even Huguccio's account of his ingenious 'embrace', with its talk of a 'debt' to a woman's pleasure, is more than a little ambiguous. It is at this point that we begin to question our picture of medieval love. For if this love was not just the slave of system-builders, it also had, one could say, a gay medical side to it. Medieval medicine did not accept that love was sinful, except in excess. True inheritor of Greek and Arab science, it expressed horror at the thought of an obstacle to nature's course. And just as it disapproved strongly of virginity as a path for women to follow, so it decreed that, to obtain happiness, the human organism must, and will, fall into the temptation of sex.

Shortly after the fall of the Roman Empire, the maps of the human body which the Classical doctors had created, where they survived, were modified by Christian thought to incorporate the latter's moral concerns.

In the seventh century the encyclopedist Isidore of Seville began to name or rename the various parts of the anatomy to express their place in the Christian scheme of things. In his *Etymologiae*, anatomy seems to be almost a word game. These names, in other words, permit an allegorical reading of each organ. The body was fitted into a cosmology simply by giving it a variety of labels.

Isidore's labels are an education in themselves. The navel, for example, is called the *umbilicus*. The root of this word is *umbos*, meaning the bossed centre of a shield; *umbilicus* also suggested the word *lumbus*, or loin. Now, according to the historians Thomasset and Jacquart, in women the navel was the centre of libido, while in men the equivalent centre lay in the loins. So the word *umbilicus*, easy to decipher for an average Latinist, evoked both the central nature of the libido to the human creature and the parallel lusts of men and women.

This term consolidated an entire tradition in medieval medicine concerning the erogenous nature of the female navel. Similarly, the word for woman, *mulier*, was intended to suggest her softness, or *mollities*. But Paul had used the word *mollities* in a disapproving way in two texts, 1 Corinthians 6 and 1 Timothy 1, where he classifies sexual sinners into four categories: *fornicarii, adulteri, masculorum concubitores* (homosexuals) and *molles* – that is, 'those who are passive', literally 'soft'.

Paul sneers at those who are the passive vehicles of another's lust, and in general at all forms of passive desire, including masturbation. The French writer Philippe Aries claims that *mollities* referred to extended erotic pleasure for its own sake – 'a repertoire of diversions for delaying coitus'. And although the Romans shared his feeling regardless of the sex of the passive party, it was inevitable that the degenerate 'softness' should come to seem female. Wasn't her nature suggested by her very name? Wasn't she soft, pliable and a temptation – a source of endless frivolous games?

As for the organs tacked by a pitying creator on to the human crux, they were *pudenda*, parts of shame, or *genitalia*, organs of generation. No opprobrium seems to surround the testicles, for they are simply named after the word for a witness, *testis*, testimony in medieval courts being valid only in twos. The term for menstruation, however, recalled the Greek word for moon, and thus allied menstrual blood with that unpredictable nocturnal body. Not for nothing do we call madmen lunatics, or the French describe the moody as 'lunatique'. Rabanus Maurus, in his *De universo*, glossed the term 'menstrual' in Isidore as follows: 'It is not allowed to approach menstruating women or to have intercourse with them, because a Catholic man is not allowed to have anything to do with the idolatry of pagans or the heresy of heretics.' The unfortunate emitters of this disgraceful blood were therefore further contaminated by a binding association with . . . Greeks.

The omissions of medicine are almost as startling as its achievements, and once again we have to report a failing with regard to the female body. For just as there was no real account of the hymen, so too the clitoris as an independent organ seems to be missing. Where was it for all those centuries? The human body as a whole was given a thorough going over by the ancient anatomists, but they nevertheless failed to get to grips with these two admittedly small and tricky devices. This does not mean that their existence was unknown, or that clitoral sensitivity had gone unnoticed. The doctors of the Middle Ages, after all, had the description of Soranus, who was translated by Moschion in the sixth century and described the female organ in matter of fact terms:

What is the woman's sinus? A nervous membrane similar to that of the large intestine: very spacious on the inside, it is, on the outside – where coitus and the acts of love take place – rather narrow; it is vulgarly called *cunnus*; outside are the labia, called *pterigomata* in Greek and *pinnacula* in Latin;

45

from the upper part there comes down into the middle what is called the *landica*.

Later, there were problems finding a specific word for 'clitoris'. When Constantine the African translated the *Al-Kunnas al-maliki* of the Arab doctor Ali ibn al-Abbas al-Majusi he 'translated' *badedera* (clitoris) in the Arabic text merely by using the Arabic word itself. Yet the exceptional sensitivity of the hidden mischief-maker was no mystery. It was mentioned by Pietro d'Abano in a work called the *Conciliator*, which otherwise devoted much of itself to the enigma of female pleasure. 'Women are driven to desire,' it says, 'by having the upper orifice near their pubis rubbed; in this way the indiscreet bring them to orgasm.'

The theologian Albertus Magnus could even recommend masturbation in young girls:

Around the age of fourteen, because of the menstrual blood and the spermatic humour descending, the thighs start to thicken, the slit in the vulva closes, the labia grow softer and thicker and a soft down springs all around: these are the signs of puberty. The girl then starts to desire coitus, but in her desire she does not emit and the more she performs the sexual act or has recourse to manual practices the more does she desire; so much so that she attracts the humour, but without emitting it. With the humour heat is attracted and, as the woman's body is cold and her pores closed, she does not emit the seed of coitus rapidly. That is why certain girls around the age of fourteen years cannot be satisfied by coitus, and if they have no partner they imagine coitus or the male member, or indulge in practices involving the use of their fingers or other instruments until their channels are opened by the heat of the friction and then the spermatic humour comes out, together with the heat that accompanies it. Thus their groins are tempered and they become more chaste. (*De animabilis*, Book IX)

We meet here the ubiquitous theory of the humours, the notion that woman is cold while man is hot, and the theory of female ejaculation, which held sway for centuries and gave promise of a certain tolerance of women's happiness. The problem of the clitoris, however, was that it was not understood except in so far as it fulfilled a clear function relative to the vagina, namely keeping out cold air. Henry de Mondeville used the old Latin term *tentigo*, which simply meant lust, and described it as 'a brawny membrane'. Avicenna and Albucasis referred to it only in its abnormally hypertrophied form, and the usual Arabic term *bazr* really defined the labia minor, not the clitoris proper. Only with Gabriele Fallopio, in the sixteenth century, was the concealed fork-shaped organ lifted out of its surrounding swaddling of tissue and bared to an astonished world. And only then was a real word found for it, one which in traditional style expressed its role in life: 'clitoris', from the Greek *klite*, or key. The 'key to pleasure' was now a reality.

Fallopio had not made any stab in the dark. His discovery was prepared for him, not by his own intuition, perhaps, but by the whole body of medieval medicine, a science which stubbornly clung to its humane curiosity. It was only a matter of time before the little fork was dug out its comfortable niche. But did anything change when it did? Did the women of Fallopio's age know more about themselves than the lovers of Troubadours? The cunning of God's architecture was certainly worthy of awed admiration, for who else could have constructed such an intricate piece of clockwork? But the purpose of this clockwork, the *reasons* the Lord had inserted this fork into the woman's vagina, these remained not less mysterious than before, but more so.

The medieval mind tended to think by analogy when faced with the inexplicable. Medicine was confronted with a mystery, the human body, which it could not otherwise decipher. And here anatomy created a picture of women that accidentally confirmed the misogynist's most cruel fantasy. Analogical thinking had led the anatomists to equate the interior of the human body with that of the pig. Since human dissections were unlawful before the fourteenth century, the doctor was free to assume that the womb of a sow and that of a woman were the same.

Anatomy manuals such as the *Anatomia porci* and the *Second Salernitan Demonstration* were based on the dissection of pigs. Arab and Greek doctors had noted that the lining of the porcine womb was covered with what the Latin translators rendered as 'hairs'. In fact, the Arabic word *layf*, itself a translation of the Greek *ine*, 'fibre', refers to any vegetable fibre and is an attempt to convey the impression of roughness inside the womb. The dissection of the sow's womb, however, confirmed the translation, for it is indeed covered with villosities. By analogy, then, it was asserted that the human womb was covered with hairs. The implications for sexual conduct were as follows: first, it was the hairs which trapped the sperm and enabled it to fuse with its female counterpart; and second, too frequent copulation would lead the female to become sterile. William of Conches, in his *Dragmaticon*, informed his readers of the total sterility of prostitutes, who, 'after frequent acts of coitus, have their womb clogged with dirt and the villosities in which the semen should be retained are covered over; that is why, like a greased marble, the woman immediately rejects what it receives'. The promiscuous woman, therefore, would not merely be spiritually abject; she would also be functionally sterile. But this creature who, insatiable as she was, could easily degenerate into a 'greased marble' was nevertheless doubly difficult to unravel rationally, because she also had a sexual drive which actually had its own proper instruments: *female testicles*.

It is one of the little known curiosities of medieval medicine that it regarded the male and female sexual organs as more or less structurally identical. Medical diagrams showing these exotic organs in a beautifully schematic and ornamental way were often interchanged one for the other – that is, the labels for the male were given in place of those for the female, and vice versa. No one seemed to notice. And no one regarded the practice as abnormal.

It was obvious that if the female possessed testes, then naturally she should be able to ejaculate. If she ejaculated, she must feel intense pleasure. And if conception depended upon her ejaculating, as doctors insisted that it did, then in order to conceive the woman had to achieve orgasm.

The tradition of female ejaculation and a female sperm had passed from the Greeks to the Arabs, and its consequences were twofold. In the first place, the arousal of the woman was given an importance it wouldn't otherwise have had. And in the second, women could participate in the prestigious mystery of the essence and origin of sperm, a substance which theologians worshipped.

For theologians, sperm were the recipients of the power of the heavenly bodies through which God exercised His action on the world. Since semen, including the female *sperma mulieris*, was the medium through which an angel deposited a human soul into matter, the mystery of its origin was prestigious. Intellectuals quarrelled over its point of origin in the body itself: did it come from the spinal column, passing through the kidneys (and thus giving us the word *renal*, which comes from the Latin *rivus*, or *stream* of semen)? Or did it come from the brain itself, being formed of blood? The Greeks called it *stagon encephalou*, or a drop of the brain, and associated its wastage with mental feebleness. Whatever its source, however, theology glorified it. It was the precious liquor, the milk of life. Thomasset notes: 'Sexuality and embryology thereby came to occupy the very heart of medieval thought, and on this topic the best authors displayed a subtlety and depth of analysis that have rarely been equalled.' Why, then, is the sexual knowledge of the Middle Ages so unknown and so despised?

The medieval period was certainly an age of love. But courtly love was not merely a beautification of frustration. The Middle Ages were incredibly promiscuous. Repression by the Church was sometimes nothing more than sheer alarm at the disruptive consequences of rampant venereal disease and hordes of illegitimate children. The bath-houses of the cities were closed down only because they were the locus of uncontrollable adultery. We forget that men and women bathed in public together, in bisexual cubicles, and that the Church had to pay for the upkeep of bastard orphans. It is the nature of that other, ideal, love that is no longer comprehensible. In the erotic games of the Troubadours there was a culture of arousal, not a so-called sexual culture, in which an exaltation of feeling was achieved by a practice of purely mental techniques. This exaltation was not spontaneous. It was formal and esoteric, difficult to master. The Countess of Die listed the permissible embraces as *tener* (holding), *ambrassar* (embracing), *baizar* (kissing) and *manejar* (fondling or caressing). All of these gentle and progressive forms of touch were controlled by the woman, for it was her fertility which would destroy the game by alerting a vengeful husband to an abnormally large belly. And at the same time, the man ceased being a provider of children. For the *trobairitz* and her lover, love was a chess-game which often ended without sex – *concubitus sine actu*, caressing without the act. Into this body of methods sex entered as a force, but not as an ideal. In itself, it was without interest. What was of interest was the penetration of another's soul. And this was to be done with the techniques not of the burglar but of the exalted, poetically gifted adulterer.

Was it possible that the *amor* of the Troubador with its acute sense of secrecy and the power of codes, its subtle psychology and techniques of deliberate postponement, could have turned the language of asceticism on its head? A huge body of erotic literature circulated about the medieval world, from books like John of Gaddesden's *Rosa anglica* and Bernard of Gordon's *Lily of Medicine*, to the tracts of the Arabs At-Tifashi and Qusta ibn Luqa. Albertus Magnus himself had wondered why it was that human species alone loves secrecy in love. Humans alone of all animals, he mused, 'arm themselves in silence and in secrecy as if going to war'. Why? Because they are aroused by secrecy itself. Secrecy is a psychological state. It is the essence of human love. Under intense pleasure, Albertus noted, the human heart contracts in exactly the same way as it does in a state of fear. Both fear and pleasure strike us dumb – and so they are linked. *Humans were aroused by their own shame.*

Shame for the ascetic, of course, was a weapon for purifying himself. But in the form of secrecy, it was, for the professional lover, an exquisite pleasure. Handbooks telling the uninitiated of the techniques of secrecy, called *Secretum secretorum*, enjoyed best-seller status, and with all this taste for secrecy, the lover had to be an expert decoder and reader of symbols. Almost every line of medieval poetry brims with these sexual innuendos – a partridge was never just a partridge, it was a disguised homosexual posing as a bird. A pear was never just a pear – it was one of Peter of Spain's twenty-six contraceptives. The reader can imagine for him or herself what a partridge in a pear tree might or might not signify, but the chances of it referring to a bird sitting innocuously in a fruit tree for normal biological reasons are utterly remote.

The European aristocracy, then, was living its

own life, reading what it wanted, largely ignoring the sexual pessimism of the scholastics. And yet this powerful class seemed unable to infect anyone else with either its courtly love or its amorous refinements. Why? Because this love was its preserve, the proof of its superiority. It was a world unto itself, and thus, though it could preserve itself intact, it could also never resist the counter-attack of misogynist and sex-hating thought which accompanied the changes of the thirteenth century. In that century, undramatic as it sounds to the modern reader, Aristotle came back into favour. And the advent of Aristotelianism dealt a death-blow to the prestige of women, of their secrets, and of their distinctive pleasures.

Aristotle was a better observer of some aspects of nature than certain of his medieval successors, and he had correctly and rationally observed that women do not, after all, ejaculate. However, as soon as this was realized, the Schoolmen (perhaps somewhat gleefully) began picking away at the prestige which the female orgasm had hitherto acquired. Now, they reasoned, this dreadful convulsion was no longer necessary; the woman emitted no seed, her pleasure was a secondary nuance, no doubt added by the Creator to make her life uncertain. The woman was a substance, as it were, on to which form was imprinted by the male. And so, even if the woman did emit sperm, this sperm wasn't as rich, active or creative as its male counterpart. Giles of Rome called it 'half-way between water and sperm'. Little more than feeble prostatic liquid. Glorified dishwater.

With female sperm devalued, there remained the thorny question of pleasure. A solution to this enigma was as ingenious as it was devious. Observing that raped women could nevertheless conceive, it had to be admitted that whatever pleasure was necessary for the emitting of the female seed could take place some time before copulation. An erotic dream could, perhaps, cause the seed to descend into place, where it would wait for the moment of penetration to be fertilized. Other theologians got more brutally to the point – thus William of Conches: 'Although in rape the act is distressing to begin with, at the end, given the weakness of the flesh, it is not without its pleasures.' A sentiment which seems to be imperishable.

The point of all this was that, if a woman could be seen as in thrall to a power she either could not control or whose charms she was incapable of refusing, so her prestige could be diminished. The doctrine of dreams was enrolled to this effect. If, as many demonologists believed, a demon could steal into a woman's head during her sleep, her control over her own fertility was instantly made unbelievable. Doctors went into fine detail concerning how these demons could actually enter the sleeping person's body through the faculty known as *phantasia*, located in the frontal lobes of the brain; once they had entered they could cause erotic images to appear there which led directly to the sexual act.

The thirteenth-century scholar Vitelo explained the role of the imagination as follows: 'It operates to a great extent during the act, and the spirits, moved by an imaginary form, suddenly run throughout the body to aid coitus.' Was this how husbands were able to impregnate their wives while separated from them by hundreds of miles? While she was committing adultery, the face of the dear departed (if not actually missed) one would suddenly appear in the wife's mind. While this in itself would normally pose only the most private of inconveniences, for the medieval woman it was a catastrophe of the first order – or a godsend, depending on the humour of the husband. For the illegitimate child which appeared nine months later would bear the husband's face and not the lover's. This elegant theory gave rise to many strange court cases in the Middle Ages, and one well-documented case as late as 1636.*

* Johann Klein, in 1698, related the case of the nobleman Jérôme Auguste de Montléon of Grenoble, whose wife bore him a son after he had appeared to her in a dream. On the advice of the physicians and midwives of Grenoble the Parliament accorded the son rights of inheritance, though the Faculty of the Sorbonne in Paris later expressed its doubts over this decision. Klein is retelling events that occurred in 1636, and he doesn't tell us the one thing which we would most like to know – did the husband actually believe her?

Erotic dreams announced conception and caused an involuntary discharge of 'ripe, white and viscous humour'. Women, therefore, could become pregnant without wanting to, without knowing what was happening and without being able to intervene. They were therefore irresponsible, mysterious and inert.

In fact, an increasing hostility to women began to make itself felt throughout the twelfth century. Women were strangely allied to disease – to leprosy, for example. Didn't Iseult taunt Tristan when he was disguised as a leper with her feminine invulnerability to it? Didn't they wreak havoc with the strictly biological purpose of sex, as laid down by the great jurists Peter Lombard and Gratian? Weren't they lethal when menstruating, able to sour milk and ruin abundant harvests merely by looking at them?

Aristotle himself increased the momentum of this hostility by his dire warnings of the fatal consequences of overdoing sexual pleasure. Since semen for him was a drop of the brain, a distinctly unpleasant connection was established between debauchery and a dreadful shrivelling of the brain. The more you ejaculated beyond your allotted quota, the smaller your brain became. Albertus recorded a case of a libidinous monk who gave up the ghost one morning after having lusted after a beautiful woman forty times before matins. The autopsy revealed, to the chastizing horror of the doctor, that the wretch's brain had shrunk to the size of a pomegranate and that his eyes, those organs so uniquely close to the brain, had practically disappeared. What greater proof could there be of the fatality of sin? Aristotle, in his *Generation of Animals*, had menacingly implied that the withering of the eyes was the particular affliction of the sybarite:

> For of all the regions in the head the eyes are the most seminal, as is proved by the fact that this is the only region whch unmistakably changes its appearance during sexual intercourse, and those who over frequently indulge in it have noticeably shrunken eyes. The reason is that the nature of the semen is similar to that of the brain . . .

Could the theologians have wished for any better authority? The terrible threat levelled against masturbating youths over the centuries has therefore an illustrious heritage, but one which was equally effective when it came to disparaging the biology of women and censuring over frequent contact with them. A quasi-medical reason shored up the purely theological one for waging war on sexual love, and gave the Church a weapon of greater intellectual power and precision.

Medieval theology's attack on sexual love was always enmeshed with its defence of procreation, the family and fertility. It had to abolish the one and glorify the other. During the Inquisition in Languedoc against the ascetic Gnostic Cathars, defendants often had to prove their faithfulness to the Church by proving that they enjoyed sex! Thus John of Toulouse, in 1230: 'I am no heretic, for I have a wife and lie with her and have children; and I eat meat and lie and swear and am a faithful Christian!' But even if in the Middle Ages what the Church really wanted was a straightforward, vigorous, heterosexual fertility which would guarantee a high birth-rate with a minimum number of bastards, means of achieving this did nothing to lessen its own tensions, which could only increase with time. Its exquisite blackmailings were the effect of its own Gnostic past, and as it undertook its crusade in defence of baby production, a fertility which had for its improbable exemplar that of a virgin, this past seeped out from within. And unfortunately for its subjects, the Church's futile and confused repression of pleasure therefore seemed as natural as sleepwalking.

Yet repression of erotic love was not the only consequence of this increase in sexual pessimism. As it grew in intensity, it threw up other, perhaps even stranger, nightmares: witches, salacious Jews and lepers. It is to these tragic and shameful figures that we must now turn.

4

The Witch

The *Malleus maleficarum*, or 'Hammer of the Witches', was written by two Dominican friars called Jacob Sprenger and Heinrich Krämer in 1486. It was intended as a handbook for Inquisitors working in southern Germany and was endorsed by Pope Innocent VIII, who had become alarmed at the supposed spread of witchcraft in the Catholic lands. The witch mania which was unleashed over the next two centuries coincided not, as scholars today love to point out, with the Dark Ages, but with the scientific revolution: one could say that its incomprehensibility is one of its most endearing characteristics.

Why did hatred of witches increase at this time?

Before the year 1230 or thereabouts the Church had dealt with isolated cases of *maleficia*, or supernatural ill-doing, but had never considered the earthly domain to be under attack from a military-style campaign by the tribe of devils. From the mid-thirteenth century, however, it began to feel less secure in its position: the Albigensian Crusade in the first decades of that century had revealed a Gnostic heresy in south-west France which had had to be quelled by limited genocide. It had carried this out by labelling the Cathars as 'witches', linking them (as it happened, not unjustly) to the redoubtable wizard Simon Magus. A century later, the reformist mission of Jan Huss in Bohemia had turned into a full-scale revolt and civil war. A mood of intensifying pessimism began to overtake many of the popes, particularly John XXII, Gregory IX and Eugenius IV, all of whom were personally terrified of witches. In his decretal letter of 1326, known as the *Super illius specula*, John was already talking of witchcraft as a 'pestilential plague'.

The great nineteenth-century historian of witchcraft Joseph Hansen argued that the Inquisition 'invented' witchcraft as an organized doctrine in the period between 1230 and 1430. The driving force behind this invention, he said, was a Church 'whose existence was threatened by heresies'. The scholastic community investigated the commerce between mortals and demons and decided that sex was the thing they most had in common. It was by sexual intercourse that the demon entered the human world, and the woman, or man, who enjoyed this intimacy was a witch. The copulating demons were classified as *incubi*, meaning those who lie on top, and *succubi*, meaning those who lie underneath, i.e. as male and female demons. Since the demon properly speaking was not sexed, these were in fact sexual *appearances*, and a demon could be male one minute and female the next. Their ingenuity was such, in fact, that a single devil could turn into a *succubus*, trap some mortal semen in its womb and then turn into an *incubus* immediately afterwards in order to inject this same semen into a woman. The result was a 'changeling' – or, in more hideous interpretations, a mentally handicapped child.

There are many conflicting theories of witchcraft. For Michelet, it was a sublimated revolt of the serf class plunged in abysmal misery and taking nocturnal revenge on the lords of the manor – a 'communion of revolt'. For the witchcraft scholar Murray, it was a persistence of the pagan cult of Diana. For others, an 'imaginary heresy'. For feminists like Claudia Honegger, a renewed repression of women. And for sociologists like Andreski, a convulsion provoked by the advent of syphilis.

One other thing: the great persecutions that took place between about 1450 and 1650 were concentrated in two alpine areas, the Alps and the Pyrenees. By far the largest number of executions took place in these two mountainous regions, comprising, in the case of the Alps, the cities of southern Germany, and in that of the Pyrenees, the territory of Languedoc. The Inquisition had been founded, let us remember, in the mid-thirteenth century to break the spine of the great heretical rebellions of the Middle Ages, that of the Cathars in Languedoc and that of the Vaudois in the Alps.

Two centuries later, witches burned in the latter region were known as *Waudenses* (Vaudois) and their gatherings as *Valdesia*, while in Languedoc they were known as *Gazarii*, which is to say Cathars.

The papal authorities made no bones about their desire to make witchcraft and heresy identical: all the witchcraft manuals written by the Inquisition make a great effort to prove that one equalled the other. There was also the isolation and racial difference of mountain people to consider: was witch-persecution a means of bringing them forcibly into the fold? Many people have seen what they call 'mountain imagery' in witchcraft, and the role of the Inquisition is equally striking. But in the end none of these explanations is ever complete. If it was a suppression of women, why were so many men executed as well? If a repression of the lower classes, why so many burghers and merchants on the pyres? If a question simply of heresy–extermination, why use witchcraft as an excuse? If a symptom of syphilis, why was it concentrated in these mountain areas?

It is true, however, that many mercenaries in syphilis-ridden armies came from poor alpine areas. No one reading the Inquisition tracts on witches can fail to be astonished at their intense (sometimes even farcically so) sexual imagery. A hidden voyeurism runs through them. The *Malleus* itself goes in extraordinary detail into the sex lives of demons and their paramours, as if the writers had actually peeped at them through keyholes (many, of course, attempted to do just this, but surprisingly they rarely saw the culprit themselves). They record hundreds of interviews with women who, they say, disclose all the salacious intimacies of their bedroom sessions with *incubi*. The tone is frequently appalled; but so also is it one of fascination. There is a grudging awe at the Devil's enormous organ. And this aspect of witchcraft, the tasting of supernatural pleasures, was by no means marginal or incidental. It was at the centre of the picture of the witch. We should forget the image of the witch as an old hag well beyond the age of copulation, although old women of the lower orders were suspected of being traffickers in abortions, aphrodisiacs and sundry sexual secrets. Usually the witch was in good sexual health. She felt desire for her demon. She could be beautiful herself. Many pictures of witches from the seventeenth century show her as equipped with superbly proportioned buttocks and Rubenesque thighs. In short, the witch was woman at her most dangerous, which is to say, at her most lascivious.

At the same time, fear of demons became paranoiac. Luther believed even the flies that landed from time to time on his body were demons spying on him. 'We are subject to the Devil,' he wrote miserably in *A Commentary on St Paul's Epistle to the Galatians*, 'both in body and in goods; for we be strangers in this world, whereof he is the prince and god.'

Was the witch an invention of the sexually

pessimistic mind fuelled by the Gnostic sentiments so obvious in this quote from Luther? *For we be strangers in this world, wherof he is the prince and god.* It is a statement with which Goya, for one, would wholeheartedly have agreed. And if we are strangers in the world, what is the witch but completely familiar to it?

There was nothing new in the magical feats of witches. The witch, in fact, like the virgin, was woman in her most magical form. In the chronicles of Ralph of Coggeshall and in the strange tales of Johan Nider's *Formicarius* (or Ant-Heap) we see her flying around like a bat, jumping out of fifth-storey windows and performing medical operations of avant-garde brilliance. In Ralph's thirteenth-century collection we read of the witch of Rheims who, after being condemned to the stake, flew out of a window aided only by a ball of string, somewhat like the fairy Melusine. Leonardo da Vinci was centuries behind her. In the pages of the twelfth-century sceptic John of Salisbury, she leaps around the darkened countryside at night shining like a glow-worm – hence her title *noctiluca*, she who shines by night, a classical synonym for Diana.

But her magic does not make her admired. On the contrary. The first reference to witches in the Middle Ages is to be found in Gratian's *Decretals* of 1140. Here the writer paints a scene straight out of Goya:

It is also not to be omitted that some wicked women, perverted by the Devil, seduced by illusions and phantoms of demons, believe in and profess themselves, in the hours of the night, to ride upon certain beasts with Diana, the goddess of pagans, and an innumerable multitude of women, and in the silence of the night to traverse great spaces of the earth . . .

The popes themselves were not slow to indulge in fantastic sexual innuendo when it came to these odd female nocturnals. In 1232, Gregory IX wrote a decretal letter to King Henry of Germany which is now known as the *Vox in Rama*. In it he describes, with barely concealed fear, loathing and fascination, the initiation ceremonies of novice witches. In the first place, he writes, they suck a toad's mouth and tongue before kissing its hind parts. They then kiss a mysterious corpse-like figure whose face is more dead than alive, and are admitted to a feast in a chamber containing a stone statue (are there here shades of the legend of Don Juan?). The initiates are then presented with a black cat, who walks around the room backwards 'with its tail erect'. They are then obliged to kiss its hind parts as well. 'When the ceremony is over the lights are put out and those present indulge in the most loathsome sexuality, having no regard to gender.'

Fifty years later, an anxious John XXII, sitting on the see at Avignon and having escaped two assassination attempts, confessed to fearing that

witches were being used as hit-squads to elimi-
nate him! In 1376 the Inquisitor Nicholas Eyremic
published his handbook *Directorium inquisitorium*, a
forerunner of the *Malleus*. In it he identified evil as
latria, or holy worship misdirected towards idols.
The notion of a *systematic* assault directed against
Christendom by Satan using all his forces had now
become explicit, and two hundred years later the
Inquisition was in full swing in its persecution of
witches. What, then, was feared in the sorceress?
That she was a heretic, an indulger in *idolatria*?
Gregory's shivers of revulsion at the thought of
these women kissing cats' backsides seems more
to the point. The witch was a kind of supernatural
whore. In one of the confessions gathered by the
Inquisition in Toulouse, a witch named Anne Marie
de Georgel told of how she was met one day by a
giant devil while doing her washing on a hill outside
the town. How did he convert her? By 'blowing
into her mouth'. The following Saturday she was
transported to a Sabbat where she submitted to
the desire of an 'enormous He-Goat' – exactly the
black and lecherous one we see in Goya – in return
for which she is taught how to make spells out of
gallows rope. The devil, it is to be noted, didn't
just shake her hand, take off his hat or say 'Good
morning' – *he blew into her mouth*. And she seems
to be willing. For how can anyone, even a devil,
blow into your mouth unless you want him to?

The *Malleus maleficarum* gathers all this sexual
suspicion into one explosive and sinister book,

the inner coherence and rigour of which only makes its surreal logic all the more fearsome. And at the centre of its brilliant demonology lay the cold-humoured, lascivious and alien hearts of the fair sex.

In Part 1, Question 6, the authors explain with great patience why it is that women are more prone to witchcraft than men. Naturally, they can't do this without enquiring into 'the general conditions of women', without, as they modestly disclaim, 'detracting from a sex in which God has always taken great glory'.

'Now the wickedness of women,' they say, 'is spoken of in Ecclesiastes XXV: 'There is no head above the head of a serpent: and there is no wrath above the wrath of a woman.' They then quote the famously misogynistic rant of Chrysostom (which really ought to be anthologized): 'What else is woman but a foe to friendship, an inescapable punishment, a necessary evil, a natural temptation, a desirable calamity, a domestic danger, a delectable detriment, an evil of nature painted with fair colours!'

The Inquisitors do note that when medieval ascetics talked of 'woman' in this way they were often simply talking of sex, for which the most convenient metaphor was the gender you practised it with. Yet the misogyny of the *Malleus* itself is beyond doubt. In fact, it is hypnotizing:

If the world would be rid of women, to say

nothing of witchcraft, it would remain proof against innumerable dangers . . .

I have found a woman more bitter than death . . . and as the sin of Eve would not have brought death to our souls and body unless the sin had afterward not been passed to Adam, to which he was tempted by Eve, not by the devil, therefore is she more bitter than death.

More bitter than death, again, because that is natural and destroys the body, but the sin which arose from woman destroys the soul by depriving it of grace, and delivers the body up to the punishment for sin.

More bitter than death, again, because bodily death is an open and terrible enemy, but woman is a secret and wheedling enemy.

It seems hardly necessary for them to add: 'All witchcraft comes from carnal lust, which in women is insatiable.'

Why do women succumb so easily to good-looking demons? Because they are lustful? Not only: they are also credulous, impressionable, have 'slippery tongues', weak memories and are 'quick to waver'. They continually boil and heave with passion. Their feebleness of mind and body make them ideal targets for wandering demonic Romeos. But above all they are more carnal: 'But the natural reason is that she is more carnal than man, as is clear from her many carnal abominations. And it should be noted that there was a defect in the formation of the first woman, since she was formed from a bent rib.' Even the etymology of her name revealed her true essence: *fe*, 'faith', and *minus* . . . the faithless one.

This established the witch as a *woman*, or rather as a force of lust. The point was that sorcery was sexual in nature. Witches were always accused of causing impotence or ruining marriages. And there were countless 'eye-witness' accounts of mating with devils, as well as many accounts left by male witches of the icy coldness of devils' wombs. The obscenities of the great demonologists were therefore perfectly in keeping with the matter in hand. Why, though, were they so mesmerized by the size of the Devil's member? We have already quoted from Nicholas Rémy, a particularly violent Inquisitor of the sixteenth century, on the Satanic member, but his *Demonolatry* hardly fights shy of going into greater detail:

And all female witches maintain that the so-called genital organs of their Demons are so huge and so excessively rigid that they cannot be admitted without the greatest pain. Alexée Drigie (at Harcourt, 10 November 1586) reported that her Demon's penis, even when only half in erection, was as long as some kitchen utensils which she pointed to as she spoke; and that there were neither testicles nor scrotum attached to it. Claude Fellet (at Mazières, 2 November 1584) said that she had often felt it like a spindle swollen to an immense size so that it could not be contained by even the most capacious woman without pain. This agrees with the complaint of Nicole Morele (at Serre, 19 January 1587) that, after such miserable copulation, she always had to go straight to bed as if she had been tired out by some long and violent agitation.

An even more vicious demonologist was Pierre de Lancre, who wrote a treatise called *Tableau de l'inconstance des mauvais anges et démons* in 1612. In this work he, too, ponders the question of the Satanic organ. After noting that the Devil likes to take pretty women from the front and ugly ones from behind, he goes on:

Margueritte, daughter of Sore, aged between 16 and 17 years, testifies that the Devil, whether he takes the form of a man or a he-goat, always has a member like a donkey, having chosen to imitate the animal which is best endowed. It is long and thick like an arm: when he wants to copulate with any of the girls or women he conjures up a bed of hay on which he makes them lie, which does not at all displease them. And he never appears at the Sabbat in any function whatsoever without having his tool outside in good shape and size. This is the opposite of what Boguet says: that the women saw him with a thing not much larger than a finger and thick in proportion. Perhaps the witches of Labourt are better served by the Satan

than those of Franche Compté . . . It appears that
this bad Demon has a half and half member: half
of flesh and half of iron, right along; and the same
is true of his testicles . . .

De Lancre dwelt on long and detailed descriptions of orgies at Sabbats and made it quite clear
where his interests lay. But there are far more
interesting questions raised by the incubus than
these speculations on the Devil's dimensions. What,
after all, *were* these horny demonic pirates hanging
around women's hair (to which they were attracted
like moths to a naked bulb) and whispering into
nuns' ears in their cells? Where, for that matter, did they come from? Why was an entire
body of literature devoted to them – to their
habits, their anatomy and their moods? And why,
come to think of it, do we assume they did
not exist? Faced with this huge body of eye-
witness evidence, shouldn't we agree with Calvin
when he says, 'Devils are not thoughts, but actu-
alities'?

The incubus began in the Judaic tradition and is far
older than most Christian theology. In the Zohar it
is related that Adam spawned the race of demons
during a separation from Eve by mating with
Lilith. The rabbis had inferred that, since Adam
was a hundred and thirty years old when Seth was
born, it must have been during this period that
he was separated from Eve. What he did during

this presumably adulterous period of refound bach-
elorhood is not clear, but that he copulated with
female spirits was more or less decided. From these
female demons impregnated by the roving Adam,
the demons are descended.

The Talmud then says that, like humans, demons
can procreate among themselves, eat, drink and
die. They can claim four mothers in the Talmudic
lore: Lilith, Naama, Igereth and Machalath – each
of whom has given birth to countless numbers
of defiled spirits. In some interpretations, these
women were the wives of Sammael, the demon-
prince; or else Naama was the sister of Tubalcain,
the mother of the devil king Aschmedai and source
of all the infernal tribe.

Lilith herself is a figure closely tied to the witch.
In the Vulgate Isaiah we find the term which came
to designate 'witch' in medieval Europe: '*lamia*'.
Isaiah 34:14 reads: '*Ibi cubavit Lamia et invenit sibi
requiem*' ('The screech-owl also shall rest there and
find for herself a place of rest'). 'Lamia' is the Latin
rendering of the Hebrew 'Lilith'. After falling foul
of Adam, Lilith became a killer of children, for
children were subject to her for eight days after
birth, in the case of males, and up to twenty in the
case of females. Is it from here that the baby-killing
reputation of the witch derives?

Lilith became an object of terror in Jewish communities. Charms were given to mother and child
just after childbirth to ward her off. Meanwhile,
the other demons had settled down in the collective

imagination. The demon leaders were thought to have their kingdoms, and their subjects were held to be sexed just like mortals. From this tradition, too, comes the claim that they make love to mortals of the opposite sex and the identification of the incubus with erotic dreams (from which we have ultimately derived our term 'incubus' for nightmare). The book *Emek Hammelech* even has Lilith passing her time pursuing men in their sleep . . .

All of this mythology of the incubus must have existed in Europe's Jewish communities, but it took several centuries for it to cross over into non-Jewish lore. Anecdotal tales of women being assaulted by leech-like demonic paramours were common, however, and in the *Life of St Bernard* we can find the saint exorcizing one from a woman who had enjoyed the company of an incubus for six years without her husband's knowledge, by means of a ceremony involving the snuffing of candles. Was sex with a devil, then, more pleasant than we are led to believe? In the well-known story of Gerbert of Aurillac the youthful Gerbert, later to be pope, meets the demon Meridiana in a lonely wood after being rejected by the object of his affection, the daughter of a provost. The demon tart is sitting provocatively on a pile of cash. The two together seduce the pope-to-be on the spot and he begins a love affair with Meridiana which lasts for years. Even when the provost's daughter eventually realizes her mistake and seduces him in a garden where she finds him asleep, he dutifully repents to Meridiana and is forgiven. It is only when he is dying, after years in papal office, that he decides to confess publicly and sever himself from her. He might have done this because he was afraid of her stealing his soul, but not necessarily so: in the early Middle Ages, the demon didn't always steal souls. In fact, people of that time seemed quite comfortable in the presence of incubi. In the *Diologus* of Caesarius of Heisterbach for example, demons are seen conversing amicably with humans and, like Gerbert and Meridiana, falling in love with each other. When Alvar Pelayo (died 1352) enumerated the vices of women he defined the one hundredth and first as their marked taste for going to bed with demons. He went on to describe a nunnery infested with them which he had been utterly unable to exorcize. 'The demons had such familiarity with some of them that they were not afraid of them, but talked with and caressed them fearlessly.'

Was Pelayo faithfully recording what he had seen? Who *were* the nuns conversing with and fondling? Can we imagine ourselves, for example, talking with and actually caressing a figment of our imaginations – not once, in the middle of the night, or during a dream, but day after day, on a quotidian basis? And yet we don't think that these nuns had nervous systems any different from our own. In the stories of Gobelinus Persona (1328–1421) there is a German knight who lived with a succubus for three years, of whom it was said that it 'talked freely with all comers, played delicately on a musical instrument, played at dice, drank wine but never allowed himself to be seen except his hands, which were tender and soft . . . After three years he departed, doing no harm.'

At first, then, the incubus was gentle and erotic. With time, he turned into a rapist, the change occurring some time during the fourteenth century, as Norman Cohn shows. The authors of the *Malleus* tell us that forty-eight women were executed in five years at Ratisbon and Constance for incubus-love, for the incubus had finally ended up posing a threat because he was seen as a conspirator, a stealer of souls. Yet even during the height of the witch-craze the old idea of the incubus seemed to lurk about in odd corners of Europe. In Venice, for example. There, in the early seventeenth century, the witch Anna de Ogniben confessed to sleeping with an incubus for three years, but she was never punished and received only the mildest of rebukes. And at the same trials one Lucietta, accused of sleeping with an incubus named Diaspontino, was also let off the hook, as if what she had done was merely in the normal course of things. The air was buzzing with demons, and it was wearily expected that women would get into trouble with them, especially as they literally let their hair down. But elsewhere the attitude to this promiscuity between two races illicited a kind of furious apartheid designed to make sure that the demon would keep away from Christian women. William of Auvergne talked of the sufferings of those subjected to demonic rape: for him, the incubus was now nothing more than a molester, a dirty old man with a prong. He had come much closer to the demons we see crouching behind the death-bed of the dying man in Goya's *St Borgia*, rather than being the suave and charming seducer with hidden little horns whom we could easily imagine flirting with Manhattan heiresses in an Ernst Lubitsch film. 'Husbands have actually seen Incubus devils swiving with their wives', the *Malleus* says in shocked tones, while elsewhere we are told that these ingenious thieves stole penises from unwary men, not as witches did, by covering the organ with a 'glamour', but by actually severing and making off with it. This operation, they inform the uninitiated, is accompanied by a certain amount of anguish. However, it was surely a good angel who made them perform this drastic art of anatomical sabotage, for 'by doing so he cuts off a great source of profit to him; for he knows that he can work more witchcraft on that act than on any other human acts'.

Incubi were invaluable to polemicists. You only had to look hard at the face of Luther, for instance, to know *immediately* that his father was one. They were also useful for explaining the extremely odd sexual behaviour of nuns. If the demon in his assumed shape was 'like a ship that the wind moves', he was also able to steal into the sleeping

mind, as we have seen. Sleeping nuns were particularly easy pickings. In 1467 Alphonse de Spina
described how nuns would be visited at night by
incubi in their sleep and, waking the next morning,
would find themselves 'polluted just as if they had
commingled with a man'. The sisters of Loudun
were hardly exceptional in this respect, although it
is never very clear *how* the demonologist comes by
his information. Was it the nuns themselves who
spread the rumour that they were being polluted
by goblin *amours*? Or did the demonologist have an
intuition, a sixth sense, which made him particularly perceptive when it came to supernatural sex?

With the sixteenth and seventeenth centuries,
demonology reached its golden age. Baroque
and splendid masterpieces of demonic sexual lore
spewed forth from the printing presses, divulging
all the secrets of the incubic anatomy. The Inquisitor Sylvester Prierias, in his *De strigimagis* of 1521,
even dissected the penises of incubi (imaginatively,
one realizes with disappointment). These perverted
extra-terrestrials, it seemed, had developed by the
early sixteenth century cunning genitals in the form
of a so-called *double penis*, or, to give it its technical
name, the *membro genitali bifurcati*. This devilish pole
actually split into two halves in mid-air and enabled
the disgusting aerial sybarite to 'abuse himself
simultaneously with both organs', an acrobatic
act whose precise technicalities were deliberately,
one feels, left a little vague. Meanwhile, in the
realm of sexual psychology, the demonologists

were making great strides forwards. Delassus, in his *Les incubes*, described the case of a girl in 1643 whose sexual organs experienced a 'violent over-excitation' whenever an incubus approached her. And Sinistrari, perhaps the most sublime of the late demon-scholars, described the case of a nun who was in the habit of locking herself in her cell after dinner without any good reason. An inquisitive sister followed her and after a while 'she heard a sound as of two voices conversing in subdued tones (which she could easily do since the cells were divided by but a light partition), then a certain noise' (the text in French actually runs '. . . *une sonorété vaginale*'). Alarmed by this creaking of the bed, the groans and sighs 'as of two lovers in an orgasm of love', she asks the Abbess to inspect the cell, but no second party is found. Undeterred, the determined spy bores a hole in the wall, 'and what should she espy but a comely youth lying with the nun, a sight she took good care to let the others enjoy by the same means'. The erring sister later confessed under the threat of torture that she had been consorting with her lovely incubus for many years, presumably using the lame excuse of after-dinner indigestion for a discreet post-prandial withdrawal.

By now, copulation with a demon had been classed as tantamount to bestiality and as such was punishable by death. Alfonsus Liguori in the *Theologia moralis* wrote: 'Sin with a succubus or an incubus is called bestiality; to which sin is added also malice against religion, sodomy, adultery and incest.' The incubus had come closer to the myths of the werewolf and the vampire, to which it is related, and to the submerged world of nightmares. But before the age of witchcraft was ended by an irresponsible and glum rash of rationalism, demonology had one last fling in the shape of two extraordinary writers: Ludovicus Maria Sinistrari de Ameno, and the ardent Johannes Henricus Pott.

Sinistrari died in 1701, and wrote his great work *De daemonialitate* in the last years of his life, though it was not published until 1875, when Isidore Liseux, the Parisian publisher of erotica, brought it out as part of their discreet 'catalogue raisonné'. Sinistrari himself was famous in the seventeenth century as a criminologist and was also one-time consultor to the Holy Inquisition in Rome. The book on demons is therefore almost certainly a part of his work in criminology, as if the demon were now little more than a sort of shifty underworld lout who could be sent off to the penal colony if caught molesting magistrates' daughters. Parts of this book are also undoubtedly intended as a confession manual for priests, who could certainly expect to run up against a few incubi in the confession box.

First, Sinistrari claims that incubi and succubi are not demons but different beings altogether. They are what are called *follets* in French, *folleti* in Italian and *duendes* in Spanish. Impelled to lustfulness, they are indifferent to exorcisms. They are capable of great sentimentality and frequently fall hopelessly in love with both men and women. These *fellati* can be born and die, can be of either sex, have human senses and passions and are made of matter, though a matter, naturally, which is 'exceedingly tenuous'. They can penetrate through substances by means of the pores which exist in all matter and can enlarge or contract at will. What is most unusual about them, however, is that they participate in the drama of redemption.

The *fellati* also organize themselves into societies, with laws and classes. They have a human-like shape and have souls, though they live longer than humans. They are driven by a pure desire for sexual gratification, requiring no renunciation of Christ nor any desecration of holy rituals. Nor are they stealers of souls. The only thing they share with the incubi of Sprenger and Krämer is their polymorphism, a virtuosity with animal disguises. Sinistrari says that a *fellato* haunted a monk of Certosa of Ticino, and when the brother proved stubborn chased him first as a skeleton, then as a hog, an ass, a bird, an angel and finally as his own confessor.

Backing for the *fellato* is sought in Jerome's *Life of St Paul*, in which St Anthony meets a small man with horns and goats' feet while wandering in a desert looking for Paul's hermitage. Jerome then tells of a similar little imp who was brought to Alexandria in the reign of Constance, his body pickled, and then taken to Antioch to be gawped at by the imperial court.

Sinistrari himself goes into detail when he describes the imp's love-life. The incubus takes care only to use the best semen available, 'abundant, very thick, very warm, rich in spirits and free from serosity'. He does this, according to Thomas Malvenda, by mating with robust men and then with robust women, 'taking care that both shall enjoy a more than normal orgasm, for the greater the venereal excitement, the more abundant the semen'. For Sinistrari, intercourse with one of them was not a crime, more a careless slip. Who could blame women if their heads were turned by these wonderfully equipped gigolos who, at the nod of a head, disappeared into thin air? As the consultor to the Inquisition tolerantly explained, they came from the lowest orders of spirits, satyrs, fauns, dryads and fauns – frisky creatures all of them, and with hardly much of an ignoble reputation. A virtuous matron of Pavia, for instance, is caressed by one with indescribable gentleness and subtlety, but none the less rejects it, upon which, in a fit of playful pique, it builds a wall around her bed. The wall gets higher and higher, until the woman and her husband are unable to get in and out of bed without the aid of a ladder. But does it haunt them, shoot arrows at them, give the matron abdominal cramps or strenuous periods? Not a bit of it. All it does is make them use a ladder to get in and out of bed. The incubus is a poltergeist, one with a certain weakness for beauty, but all the more human for that. The demon is no longer demonized.

Why, then, was this incredible collective fantasy needed? Sinistrari's contemporary Henricus Pott didn't know the answer any more than Sinistrari. Both of them were under the interesting delusion that they were describing something endemic to nature, much as one would describe the phrenology of criminals or the electrical charge in frogs' legs. Pott, however, was genuinely in awe of his subject. Demons, even as late as this, were not funny. In the sombre (and splendidly titled) *Specimen juridicum de nefando lamarium cum diablo coitu* of 1689 he affirmed that incubi outnumbered succubi, as if he had actually counted them; that man is possessed by a spirit of fornication which attracts him to lust as a magnet to iron; and that witches give birth to worms which they inject into people's limbs. Not only that, but incubi themselves are lusty zoophiles. There is the case of the boy in Flanders born of a demon and a cow who grew up as a normal God-fearing Christian but who had an irrepressible desire to chew cuds, walk in the fields and browse with the cows.

Elsewhere, Pott quotes from Strozzi Cicogna's *Palagio degli innocenti*, a collection of witch stories which appeared in 1605. Cicogna relates the story of Margaret of Essingen whose belly swelled up after she slept with an incubus. So big did this belly become that it covered her from head to foot until she became one big walking ball and from inside her, like voices in a cave, 'came the crowing of cocks, the barking of dogs, bleating of sheep . . . etc.'. 'What the result was,' Pott meditates fearfully, 'is not stated.'

Hair-raising questions arise from these accounts. How many demons were there exactly? The sceptic Johan Weyer in 1563 counted seventy-two princes and 7,405,926 underlings. But rationalists like Balthasar Bekker and the theologian Pierre Bayle, who finally demolished the pretensions of the demonologists, never asked what the demon was, because they knew he was, in observable terms, nothing. And yet he existed. The experience of possession was not imaginary. Jean-Joseph Surin, the exorcist of the Ursuline Sisters at Loudun in 1635, has left a remarkable letter which he wrote to Father Daitichi of Rennes on 3 May of that year, in which he describes what it was like to feel one of them enter one's body:

> I have entered into combat with four of the most powerful and malicious Demons of Hell. Me, I say, whose infirmities you know; God has permitted the combats to be so violent, and the contacts so frequent, that the least of the battlefields was the exorcism . . . for three and a half months, I am never without a Devil at my side, exerting himself. Things have gone so far that God has permitted, for my sins, I think, something never seen, perhaps, in the Church: that during the exercise of my ministry

the Devil passes from the body of the possessed person and coming into mine, assaults me and overturns me, shakes me and visibly travels through me, possessing me for several hours like an energumen. I would not know how to explain to you what occurs inside of me during this time, and how this Spirit unites with mine, without depriving me either of knowledge or of the liberty of my soul, while nevertheless making himself like another me, and how it is as if I had two souls, one of which is deprived of his body, or the use of its organs, and stands apart, watching the actions of the one who has entered. Two Spirits battle on the same field, which is the body, and the soul is as if it were divided; following one part of itself, it is the subject of diabolical impressions; following the other, of movements which are all its own . . .

How do we interpret this today? Schizophrenia? Mass hysteria? The Loudun case was doubly curious in that after Urbain Grandier, the man who had persuaded the nuns to fake their possession by devils, was burnt at the stake for fraud, the nuns themselves *did* succumb to possession. That possession took the form of the Sisters going into sexually obscene convulsions, begging to be raped and pouring pornographic language over the men around them. Not only that, the possession passed to the exorcist himself! The priest watches the

demon enter him as he would watch a burglar pot-
ter around in his kitchen. What was he watching?
Who was the intruder forcing him into one half of
his own house? Are we in any position at all to say
that he was 'dreaming', or that a neurosis made him
feel and see things?

Historians always have fistfuls of theories about
witchcraft. We can certainly point to things which
seem relevant, such as, to take one example, the
misogynistic theory of menstruation, which would
seem to tell us something about the reasons for
throwing people on to bonfires. But does it tell us
anything, in the end? It is interesting to learn that
women and witches were equated with the basilisk,
a reptile which was born by parthenogenesis from a
cock's egg. We are almost certainly curious enough
to ask why a cock should lay an egg. We will learn
that a superfluity of poisonous matter from the
kidneys and genital organs of that animal remained
harmfully in its system until an *egg* formed. *Where*
did the egg form? In the cock's intestine. And what
does this have to do with witches or women? Well,
the animal which hatched out of that egg was an
innovation, a creature made of poison, hatched by
a male and crawling out of an intestine, and it had
the power to kill things merely by looking at them.
It did this by poisoning the air around them. So did
menstruating women, and so did witches.

Does this give us an insight into the imagination
of those who killed witches? The witch was most
dangerous when she *looked* at you; likewise, the

woman 'in her flowers' could tarnish a mirror by looking into it, ruin crops, sour the must of grapes, kill herbs, prevent cereals from sprouting, make trees lose their fruit, make iron rusty, blacken bronze, give rabies to dogs and dissolve the glue of bitumen, which even iron could not break down.

The woman during her period could do all the things which the witch could do, and both of them were indistinguishable from the nefarious basilisk. Did not Innocent VIII himself give a long, identical, catalogue of the things harmed by the witches' gaze? All three emitted venom through their eyes. If any of them looked at themselves in a mirror they could die instantly. Albertus explained that the eye was soaked in toxic menstrual fluid which then 'infected' the air around it; the air then transmitted the disease which had been discharged like a vapour from the eyes, and it was this which dulled the mirror's surface (and gave cot-bound infants heart trouble). Aristotle stated categorically that bleeding females turned mirrors black, and the *Malleus* talked endlessly of the power of witches to 'infect' air from their eyes, for, as it says, 'there is great power in the eyes, and this appears in all things'.

But are we any the wiser? We do learn that women were inextricably linked, by their very internal machinery, with disease. We also learn that the gaze is the most dangerous thing about a woman. It can literally kill you, as well as dissolving the glue of bitumen. But the man is also inevitably reminded of the power of that gaze to ensnare and seduce. Isn't it this which really makes her like a basilisk? And what 'infection' was he thinking of when he compared the menstruator to a leper? Did he really think he would die if he breathed in her face? It is impossible to re-create the living organism which all these beliefs went to make, just as it is impossible to know what went through the mind of a monk who never for a moment actually touched a woman, but who believed she might cause his heart to stop merely by casting a glance at him. And it is equally impossible to know what Jean-Joseph Surin experienced on 3 May 1635 when a demon passed through his body. Still less can we imagine the feelings of a 'possessed' sixteenth-century nun writhing on the floor of a cell in the grip of a beautiful incubus. No theory of witchcraft brings us closer to any of these things, any more than criminological statistics bring us into the mind of a Nielsen or a Christie. It is a vacuum which cannot be filled. Nor do the documents help us greatly. The most moving letter ever left by a 'witch' was that written to his daughter by the Burgomeister of Bamberg, Johannes Junius, who was tortured and burned in 1628. What does the letter tell us? That the Inquisition picked its victims at random. That a witch could be a powerful, religiously orthodox middle-aged male with not a stain on his record, regardless of everything we have said about menstruation and misogyny. Similarly, we can discover that the first woman tried for copulation with a demon was Lady Alice Kyteley at Kilkenny in 1324. But as we sift through the court records, all we discover is that the charge of witchcraft was fabricated by her enemy, the prosecutor Richard Ledrede, Bishop of Ossory, for purely social reasons. The phenomenon of witchcraft, it appears, covered a bewildering variety of tensions, whether the Lady did or did not sleep with an incubus in the shape of a giant Negro with an iron bar.

We can only retreat into the scepticism of Cyrano de Bergerac in his sarcastic and witty polemic against witchcraft of 1654, the *Lettre contre les sorciers* 'I have almost never,' Cyrano says, 'been told a story about Witches which did not ordinarily take place less than three or four hundred leagues away . . .'

Witchcraft, of course, is still alive and well. And there is evidence, too, that the incubus is still with us, however much the guardians of public morality and the tribe of censors stubbornly deny his presence. And we are not talking in a roundabout way about the unconscious. Recently, a Manhattan television cable station hosted a phone-in service for haunted citizens. Sure enough, dozens of desperate women rang in to claim that they were being molested by devils wanting sexual favours from them. They followed them around the house, whispered in their ears in bed, followed them to the supermarket and generally made their lives miserable. The medium on call looked completely unsurprised. 'Yes, dear,' she kept advising, 'they're a nuisance, but I'll give you my advice: if a demon is getting on top of you, literally, the best thing you can do is put on a set of red underwear. Do that, and you'll never see another one again . . .'

5

The Leper

After the witch, it was probably the leper, or his alter-ego the syphilitic, who struck the greatest terror into the sexually pessimistic imagination. Indeed, the whole story of syphilis, which now has to be told, is nothing if not a chapter in the history of that imagination. At first, it does indeed seem a morbid and unpromising affair. Yet few people remember that syphilis began life not as a virus but as a shepherd, and that he was as much a creature of fancy as the swains of any pastoral.

The unfortunate tender of flocks was dreamed up by a sixteenth-century doctor and poet, Girolamo Fracastor, whose elegant poem *Syphilis sive morbus gallicus* was published in 1530. In it, Syphilis is the shepherd of King Alcithous who one day rudely decides to overturn the altars of the Sun on the hill where he tends his flocks. He does this in order to set up alternative altars for his master; but whatever Alcithous may have thought of this faithful gesture, the Sun was infuriated by it and, for punishment, visited upon the shepherd a new disease of his own devising: a disease as innovative as it was complex. Complex, because syphilis (as the thing now became known) had an astonishing variety of symptoms, and became, in its pathological old age, a wily and cunning customer.

Fracastor was a clever doctor who in a later work guessed that the dreadful affliction was in fact caused by a multiplication of 'tiny invisible living things', which fairly accurately describes the reality, such as we now understand it. But earlier, in 1530, the Sun seemed as good a bet as any, and with it, a baleful conjunction of stars. Indeed, proper astrologers went further: the disease, according to them, had been caused by a conjunction of Saturn and Jupiter in the sign of the Scorpion and the House of Mars on 25 November in the year 1484, which led to the first great syphilis epidemic of 1495. Dürer even executed a woodcut for a poem about epidemics by Theodoricus Ulsen which shows a zodiac above the sufferer's head and that very date inscribed next to it. And if it was not the stars, then surely it was the Moors, the coupling of men and monkeys, or Spaniards mixing the blood of lepers with Greek wine. Only after a few years did another possibility suggest itself, namely the pox-ridden ships of one Christopher Columbus.

Fracastor brilliantly described the essence of syphilis, which, when considered anthropomorphically, is something of a spiv, a burglar, a card-sharp.

He is, for example, an expert in secret manoeuvres and deft deceptions. The French version from the Latin by Barthélemy says:

Chose étrange! ce mal, introduit dans le corps,
Parfois avec lenteur se trahit au-dehors,
Et souvent, sans qu'il donne un signe manifeste,
La lune, quatre fois, forme son pleine céleste:
Il se cache, il hésite, il couve sourdement . . .

(What a strange thing! This illness, once introduced into the body / Sometimes only manifests itself slowly / And often, without him giving any outward sign whatsoever / Four full moons come and go / He hides himself, hesitates, hatches his plots silently . . .)

In other words, syphilis is a slippery underworld crook. And since we know that the force of this affliction declined gradually over its first hundred years, one can only imagine the tortures inflicted upon his namesake by the sadistic Sun. In those early days, after all, the first appendage of the body to drop off was not the penis, but – infinitely worse – the nose; so much so that soon after the 'pox' reached Japan in 1512 the inhabitants of the archipelago had invented a stern saying for their errant sons: 'From your parents' eyes, you, son, conceal yourself: you will lose your nose!'

Syphilis was not only a tricky customer in the

medical sense, however. He was also a controversial one. Consider the acrimonious debate over his origins. This debate is already five hundred years old, and is about only one thing: did syphilis come from the Americas with Columbus or Torres – that is, from the land of milk and honey and the Noble Savage – or has it always existed in the Old World, much like the leprosy with which it was always associated?

The two sides have been drawing up their battle-lines since the first Spanish colonial anthropologists gave differing accounts. In the early years of this century the controversy fell into the hands of two German professors, named Iwan Bloch and Karl Sudhoff. Bloch represented the views of what had now become known as the Americanists (i.e. those who believed in an American origin), while Sudhoff stood for the opposition, or anti-Americanists.

Rather like the farcical mental duellists Professors Philifor and Anti-Philifor in Gombrowicz's *Ferdydurke*, the two leaders haggled over texts, ancient bones and biblical innuendos, and neither scored a decisive victory. Indeed, the debate still rages, although recent evidence has started to weight the scales in favour of the Americanists.

This obscure scholarly wrangling over the origins of the disease has always been passionate, and occasionally fully hysterical, because a kind of blame still attaches to those who first incubate a plague. An early defender of the American

Indians like Las Casas, for example, saw himself as defending their spiritual and racial honour by denying their 'responsibility' for syphilis; and today, revisionists of the Columbus story similarly do their best to prove that all diseases are the poison of colonizers, namely Europeans. When civilization itself is fashionably conceived of as a 'disease', as it now routinely is, this becomes inevitable. But in the end, all that is revealed is the nostalgic pessimism of the writer. And what the pessimist needs for his sense of sanity is above all a vision of moral virginity – a virginity which he finds in the Noble Savage. In 1826 the anti-Americanist Devergie became so indignant at the slightest suggestion that the gentle aborigines could have nurtured in their bodies anything so vile and hideous as a venereal disease that he claimed the whole Americanist argument had been devised 'in spite, spread in a spirit of prejudice and dishonesty'. After Rousseau, it seemed, the Noble Savage was untouchable, as to a certain extent he still is.

The historian of medicine Mirko Grmek has shown that the snail-like lesions on the bone which venereal syphilis characteristically leaves behind cannot definitely be proved to exist in any skeletons outside of the Americas before the year 1500, though several examples appear to have been found in the Americas which are dated to before that year. But in the end the protagonists are not concerned with the latest evidence of osteo-archaeology. Such things impinge little upon the minds of those who see the destruction of the native cultures of the Americas as itself syphilitic in character. We think of diseases in a violent and primitive way. They *are* a supernatural condemnation. The shame of syphilis does, after all, have to do with astrology, with a vengeful Sun, a wrathful Jehovah. For what has disease ever been if not the stigmata of a mysterious punishment, a flaying of the reprobate by a watchful God?

This is why the origins of syphilis matter so much. It is also why the story of a disease is never just the history of a pathology; it always turns out to be another story altogether, the story of an inexplicable *doubt*.

The anti-Americanists were also known as Unitarians, because they believed that syphilis is only one virus; this single virus is named *treponematosis*.

Like all viruses, they say, it is very ancient, perhaps millions of years old. It had its origins in equatorial Africa, where it remained submerged and quiet until it was spread into the Middle East in the Bronze Age by the black slave trade along Egyptian trade routes.

Today we have four variants of this virus. They are *endemic treponema*, or non-venereal syphilis; *yaws*, the African variety; *pinta*, the South American version; and finally the venereal villain, *treponema pallidum*, which was discovered only as recently as 1905 by Schaudinn and Hoffmann.

We know that by the first millennium BC

malaria, smallpox, leprosy and typhoid had come to roost in the human organism. We know also that gonorrhoea was with them, and that tuberculosis can be traced back to the Stone Age. Viruses can lie dormant for millennia before some new human expansion brings people into contact with it. As for the virus itself, it is a protean being, with an intelligence and a zest for life which scientists frankly admire. The fact that they live by human suffering is only in the nature of things, and no reason not to admire their ferocious energy. The virus is Nature at her most inventive, playful and subtle, and its cunning for disguises and adaptation, for example, enables it actually to change itself to keep pace with social habits.

No one knows if the Unitarian theory describes the true origin of syphilis, but it does go on to explain that, as the human species becomes more aware of the need for hygiene to combat disease, the wily bacillus changes tactics, concentrating always on the means of transmission which are still open to it. With time, this inevitably comes down to sexual love. For whatever the elaborate rules laid down as early as Leviticus for ritual cleanliness in the matter of genital and other diseases, sexual love is the most difficult of intimacies to control. This does not mean, of course, that all diseases are transmitted sexually, but only that some have cleverly chosen to opt for this convenient channel.

The Unitarian sees syphilis everywhere in the ancient world. Did not syphilis exterminate the twenty-four thousand worshippers of Baal Peor after their whoredom with the daughters of Moab in Numbers 25? Doesn't the long treatment of disease in Leviticus itself refer to the vagrant 'pale' syphilis? Leviticus certainly played a part in instilling in Christians an extravagant fear of sexual infections, for the unclean man described in that book as suffering from a genital discharge contaminates everything around him. His bed is infected, his clothes are infected, anyone who even touches his hand is infected. His *saliva* is deadly. 'The woman also with whom man shall lie with seed of copulation, they shall both bathe themselves in water, and be unclean until the even.' Such is the uncleanliness of the sufferer that he can escape his doom only by sacrificing turtledoves and pigeons at the tabernacle – or by disappearing into the desert.

The biblical kingdoms had early discovered the efficacy of the ultimate threat against diseased lovers: isolation. Quarantine was the standard treatment of venereal disease in the first millennium before Christ, alternating with occasional mild genocide. 'Thus shall ye separate the children of Israel from their uncleanliness; that they die not in their uncleanliness . . . This is the law of him that hath issue and of him whose seed goeth from him, and is defiled therewith.' In Numbers 31, the faithful only had to recall, the Midianite women were massacred wholesale when they were found to be *unclean*.

It is not impossible that *yaws*, in the course of time, turned itself spontaneously into venereal syphilis. But the signs of all the skin diseases known to ancient and medieval were hopelessly confused with each other. Does Avicenna describe syphilis with its lesions, or urticaria, which has almost identical early symptoms? And were the Midianite women not dispatched because they had another disease, such as gonorrhoea? For if the true syphilis was not around to torment Moses, the equally terrible gonococcus was. Not only that, but ancient man, unrepentantly promiscuous, was the gallant host of a magnificent array of sexual diseases, from the relatively mild *candida albicans* to the bizarre and gruesome *lymphogranuloma venereum*, or genital elephantiasis.

Was the profligacy of venereal disease in the ancient Near East one of the reasons for the severity of the law of Moses as revealed in Leviticus? Right at the beginning of the patristic tradition these ailments were not seen as an accident of personal misfortune, over which one had no control. They were seen as diseases of the soul as well as of the body, as punishments of the unjust.

Gonorrhoea by the year 1495 was an old, if mistrusted, friend. The word 'clap' comes from the French *clappoir*, meaning a large boil. It first appears in a manuscript of John of Arderne of 1378; but by then the 'clap' had attracted a host of expressive names: *la chaude-pisse* or, even more poignant, *ardeur de urine*. It was also known as *infirmitas nefando*, the hidden disease.

But when syphilis was first described in the 1490s, what shocked its observers was its newness, its dangerous unfamiliarity. This was not gonorrhoea, leprosy or the plague. It was not the *sahaphati* described by Avicenna and which the anti-Americanists naively claimed was syphilis. The earliest syphilis documents state unequivocally that it was something else altogether. The doctors had never seen anything like it, and none of their books, Arab or Greek, had prepared them for it. It seemed like a thunderbolt from the heavens.

In the spring of 1495, a Sicilian doctor working in Barcelona named Nicolas Squillacio wrote a letter in Latin to his friend Ambroise Rosato, another physician. In this letter, the oldest known written reference to syphilis, he says:

> The signs of the sickness are these: there are itching sensations and an unpleasant pain in the joints; there is a rapidly-increasing fever; the skin is inflamed with revolting scabs, and is completely covered with swellings and tubercules which are initially of livid red colour, and then becomes blacker. After a few days the sanguine humour oozes out; this is followed by excrescences which look like tiny sponges which have been squeezed dry . . . the disease infects neighbouring regions largely by means of contact

between men and women: this is how it recently invaded innocent Spain.*

Squillacio says that the plague came from France, and talks of 'storms in a threatening sky'. This reflects, perhaps, only the fact that the disease was already being called the *morbus gallicus*, or French sickness. But the reasons for this lie not in a true French origin but in the political crisis of the day, namely the invasion of the Kingdom of Naples by a French army under their king, Charles VIII.

The siege of Naples by the French in 1495 was the match that lit the powder keg. On 6 July in that year the two sides fought a battle at Fornovo, at which numerous Spanish mercenaries were engaged on both sides. It is known that these Spaniards were partly from Barcelona and that a few of them had accompanied Columbus to America. Present at this battle also were two Venetian doctors, named Marcellus Cumano and one Benedetto, who have left descriptions of syphilis among the troops. According to Benedetto:

Through sexual contact, an ailment which is

* It should be noted that the assumption that syphilis was transmitted through intercourse was sometimes challenged. Antonio Scanaroli of Modeno in his *Disputatio de morbo gallico* claimed that it appeared *de novo* in the genitals of both old men and virgins, making it seem as mysterious as cancer.

new, or at least unknown to previous doctors, the French sickness, has worked its way in from the West to this spot as I write. The entire body is so repulsive to look at and the suffering is so great, especially at night, that this sickness is even more horrifying than incurable leprosy or elephantiasis, and can be fatal.

Performing an autopsy on the body of a woman who had died of it, he noticed tumorous bones suppurated to the marrow and the loss of eyes, hands, teeth and nose. Within months, terror had gripped the entire Italian peninsula.

Whenever a new disease appears, it creates a literature of its own. Later, tuberculosis in the nineteenth century was to spawn a whole way of life, as Susan Sontag has shown, as well as an artistic temperament to go with it. Poets were expected to be thin, sickly, and to burn with a sort of tubercular fire. Didn't Théophile Gautier once famously declare that in his youth he could never have taken seriously a lyric poet who weighed more than ninety-nine pounds? One can well imagine the sensations caused by the Princess Belgiojoso flaunting her languorous TB on the Grands Boulevards, and inflicting upon the bourgeoisie an acute embarrassment at their own good health. With syphilis it was the same, except that the purpose of the metaphors used was completely different. For whereas tuberculosis was the sign of a sensitive, refined spirit, and a finely heightened sensuality (the model was Marie Duplessis, the Camille of Dumas and Verdi), syphilis was the sign of the reverse – of a debauched coarseness. If the TB sufferer had what Sontag calls 'an interior décor of the body' which was tasteful, the syphilitic was like a fake Second Empire bedroom complete with trashy bibelots and a tart's dressing table. In both cases, however, the body's 'internal décor' suited the inner character of the victim. The disease was the man.

The literature of syphilis rarely took the trouble to ennoble the sufferer of such internal vulgarity. It is true that in the eighteenth century Casanova could boast of the worldly scars left behind by his syphilitic chancres as if they gave him a varnished look, like an old painting. In his letters to Louis Bouilhet, Flaubert also takes time to display his *amorous wounds*, as Casanova had called them: for just as a soldier has wounds on his body, so too does a lover, and he should be proud of them because it proves his experience. 'A slight induration remains,' Flaubert wrote, 'but that is the hero's scar. It just adds to its poetic quality. One can see that it has lived, that it has weathered misfortunes. That gives it a fateful and doomed air which cannot but please the contemplator.'

Maupassant, for one, jumped for joy: 'I've got the pox! At last! The real thing!' And in those floral dreams of Des Esseintes in *A Rebours* the hallucinating hero – gazing at his rare plants, which seem to him to be Nature's way of copying the insides of animals' bodies – ends by sighing 'There is nothing but syphilis.' And this syphilis is a bloody-mouthed, greedy-eyed Nemesis.

For Des Esseintes, syphilis was not so much a normal human disease as a condition of nightmarish nature, a moral poison. And although a knowledge of the natural causes of disease has been familiar since the end of the Middle Ages, the superstition that disease itself is more than a mere pathology – that it is a moral degeneration – has never died. On the contrary, it is now returning to favour.

The belief that disease has a psychological or spiritual root is now part of the rise of a modish distrust of science. Since Wilhelm Reich, it has become virtually routine for cancer, for example, to be described as a disease of the emotions – an illness of the depressed, the humourless and the sexually repressed. The mystic sexual optimism of Reich demanded that all disease be cured by unrestrained love-making, and in a similar vein Norman Cousins wrote a best-seller, *Anatomy of an Illness*, in which he described curing himself of a terminal illness by watching Marx Brothers videos.

The scientific idea of a disease as something to which no blame can attach, which is random and enigmatic, cannot satisfy a craving for both certainty and immortality. Reading diet-cure manuals which promise remedies for everything from intestinal spores to heart disease by eating bulgar and celery root, one sometimes feels the presence of a curious hysteria, an indignation at death by something as arbitrary and irrational as disease. If you live correctly, you will live for ever – or almost. The medieval notion of disease as a moral punishment is therefore being revived. Eat badly, kill animals, live in an industrial system which damages the environment, *and you too will die* . . .

As Sontag says, cancer is now fashionably seen as a 'rebellion of the injured ecosphere: Nature taking revenge on a wicked technocratic world' – as the price, that is, of a lifestyle. The demonization of disease seems to be beginning all over again, with the simple difference that whereas in the past it was the witch and the demon who punished the sinner with illness, it is now lifestyle which does so.

What is the real source of this disillusionment on the part of people who are the first in history not to have the nauseating stench of disease constantly in their noses? A romantic anti-industrialism bolstered by two centuries of indignant poetry? Or a yearning for a personal relation to disease? Is it not really the case that what is missed is the sense of power over death which magic creates or which behaviour in inexplicable ways guarantees? By giving disease a spiritual substance, you can control it *telepathically* . . .

What are the implications of this for sexual diseases? If disease is mystified, demonized and made internal to the spiritual machinery of the individual, isn't sexual disease transformed from a neutral force of nature into a *curse*? Isn't the biblical imagination revived? One of the most depressing symptoms of an unbridled adoration of the pre-scientific and the pre-industrial is that its nightmares begin to return, but not in the forms that one expects them to. The West adored Gandhi because he sustained its self-doubting romanticism. But who remembers that Gandhi, that champion of the medieval mind, argued with passionate intensity for the abolition of hospitals in India on grounds which the Inquisition of the Middle Ages would ardently have sympathized with: that disease is a punishing demon descended from Heaven to crush the immoral? It is right for the diseased to suffer and die. It is immoral to cure them, for they are paying for their sins.

'Passions,' says Kant in the *Anthropologie* of 1798, 'are cancers for pure practical reason and often incurable.' And is not restlessness, passion, disturbance supposed to be the hallmark of the unhappy Western soul when compared to the serene, motionless contentment of the Oriental? Right at the beginning of the modern history of venereal disease, the disorder itself was seen as a demonic affliction in all ways appropriate, for instance, to the violence of the Conquistadores, though not to the happy placidity of the Noble Savage. The very man who coined the term *morbus venereus*, or venereal sickness, in 1527 – Jacques de Berthencourt – stated clearly that in his opinion the disease was a chastisement of the promiscuous

and the 'passionate'. It was named, after all, after
the dangerous goddess who inspired the original
crime. Ambroise Paré made it quite clear that the
epidemic had been instigated by 'God's wrath,
which allowed this malady to descend upon the
human race, in order to curb its lasciviousness and
inordinate concupiscence'.

In the seventeenth century, in an atmosphere of
increased puritanism, the demonic origin was even
more fiercely stated. One doctor, Jean-Baptiste
Lalli, declared: 'The searing droplets of this cruel
sickness fall on those who are hot with love and
dirtied with lust; it is a punishment for their
mistakes and their shameful desire'; and Sieur de
la Martinière, who described himself as 'médecin
chimique et opérateur' of Louis XIV, declaimed:

> It is a sickness which is worse than any suffered
> by the beasts, which in my opinion is sent to
> human beings as a curse to punish them for that
> filthy and dishonourable act which, according to
> Plato, makes the souls of men, after the death
> of the body, like those of donkeys, which are
> animals symbolic of lust. (*Traité de la maladie
> vénérienne*, 1644)

Even a hundred years later, when pleasure and
the non-lethal nature of syphilis had momentarily
asserted themselves, a young doctor named Joanne-
Francisco-Renato de Parfourru in a medical treatise
submitted to the faculty at Caen in 1772 could

complain: 'Alas too tempting desire . . . what are you playing at in fashioning new monsters for the ruination of men? O most happy ancestors, thrice happier than we! You had not discovered in the very source of life a cause of death to treacherously threaten your days.' (This treatise has the admirable title *Must we take account of the solubility of mercurial compounds in order to evaluate their antivenereal powers?* and uses a language unconsciously reminiscent of the Gnostics. It is quoted by Quetel in *History of Syphilis*.)

That the witch and the demon were the true causes of disease is well known; every illness, in fact, could be reduced to an aetiology which was *magical*. And even as the eighteenth century wore on and science began to offer more pleasing explanations, the unfortunate tendency to see disease and victim as one and the same did not disappear. The famous doctor Deidier claimed to have discovered tiny, monstrous worms in the patient which could hatch eggs and multiply like insects, but at the same time could not resist talking of 'the true scourge of that vile carnality'. Whether the sickness was seen as a kind of corrosive acid, or the result of magnetic friction, an aura of pessimism clung to the syphilitic. It was no less than inevitable that someone should eventually apply Mesmer and the laws of electricity to the problem of the French sickness; and so it was that the terrifying myth of contagion by magnetic friction arose. The electricity released by the friction of kissing, rubbing or even the fluttering of eyelids could hurl the microbe into the uninfected's body. It is difficult to imagine the naked fear of eighteenth-century aristocrats desperately trying not to blink within ten feet of another person, or watching with one open eye for flying sparks while kissing their beloved. But by then the demonization of disease had become so natural that the primeval fear of pollution by quasi-magical means (for even electricity in the hands of Mesmer had something magical about it) was impossible to overcome. Syphilis had become a kind of uncontrollable manifestation of one's own passion.

The demonization of passion had another, unexpected, side to it. Like the demonization of the diseased, it could actually glorify the sufferer. In the Middle Ages, it was not uncommon for ascetics to envy lepers, and fondly call them *pauperes Christi*, as if they were a chosen band. It was also commonly assumed that the person suffering leprosy would expiate his sins sooner than anyone else and so would be promoted more quickly in the celestial hierarchy. This envy of lepers is bizarre, and even more so when it is remembered that it was the leper's suffering that was envied . . . the laceration of his flesh.

This is why, although the leper was shunned and segregated, particularly from the twelfth century on, he was also admired. Leper-kissing became a fashionable religious exercise indulged in by the nobility; Saint-Louis asked his knights to kiss the lesions of Jerusalem's lepers, and Eleanor of Aquitaine did the same herself. It is true that when the leper went into seclusion he was effectively declared dead to the world (the Last Rites were read over him while he lay in a mock grave beneath a black shroud suspended between two trestles) and that lepers were also periodically massacred (the most spectacular pogroms being those in France in 1321 following the Poitiers edict in that year prescribing the oppression of lepers). But generally the attitude towards lepers was highly ambivalent. His disease may have been demonized, but that did not necessarily turn him into a demon. A feeling of awe surrounded him. He was a magical object.

The question posed by syphilis, however, is why the same feeling of charity and awe did not apply to the syphilitic. Andreski has pointed out that syphilis and puritanism arrived in Europe more or less concurrently. For a long time, in fact since the ancient world, lepers had been seen as satyrs – people in every way venereal in character. Aretaeus says that leprosy was often called *satyrisasis* by ancient doctors, and Galen added that this was so because the leper's face looked like a satyr's. Imaginary vices were therefore imputed to the wretched leper, a link probably enforced by the similarity of venereal diseases like genital elephantiasis and the swelling of the penis associated with leprosy. The latter led in the Middle Ages to absurd rumours about the gigantic size of lepers' organs, a characteristic they were unlucky enough to share with Old Nick. When this was added to the conviction that leprosy was transmitted sexually, the sexual demonization of the leper was complete. And yet people carried on kissing their hands. It would not have occurred to any nobleman of the sixteenth century to atone for his sins by kissing the hand of a syphilis sufferer, for the new disease was not only unapproachable – it attracted a fundamental disgust which was as new as the contagion itself. The whole delicate and precarious relation between the healthy and sick was thrown off balance. And what was it that threw this order out of kilter if not the syphilitic's slavery to Venus? The leper may have been a satyr, but the slave of Venus was something worse: a half-ridiculous proof of the sinfulness of Eve. The proof that love kills.

Ever since the rise of puritan society, there has been anguish at the thought that sexual love and mercantile trade might be incompatible. Although the hostility between religious law and love is as old as Gnosticism, the hostility between modern commercialism and love dates only from the age of syphilis, leading to today's familiar, tortured question: is love possible in a mercantile culture? But Tokugawa Japan and Sung China were mercantile cultures and there was no breakdown there. For that matter, early capitalist northern Italy was also a rigorous mercantile culture, and its hedonism and cultivation of love were outstanding. The Florence of Cavalcanti was a merchants' bee-hive. There is no inevitable link between profit and repression, but in modern Europe this repression nevertheless occurred. As the industrial age matured in the nineteenth century, the previous demonization of passion turned to the artist's advantage, and the full opposition of passion and the work ethic reached its apogee. The middle classes were thrust into the strange predicament of working hard in their businesses by day and swooning to *Tristan* by night. The artist, bearer of a mysterious disease which he tried to spread to others, suddenly begins to despise the wealth-creating class which feeds him. And by some deeply rooted instinct for a higher existence, they in turn start to imitate him by despising themselves.

Denis de Rougemont has shown how our notion of a 'profane' love derives from the northern mystics, who inherited it from Gnosticism. It is this mysticism which underlies the modern novel and music, with their cult of pathological passion. But the precise character of the money-making puritan who is now so unfashionable (because the propaganda of passion has been so successful) cannot be explained away, as it usually is, as that of a life-hating machine whose entire being is dedicated to accumulation and conquest. It was in the early sixteenth century that the lover came to look like the leper, and the culture of family and work founded upon a tough sexual pessimism came to triumph. Why did this happen?

We have seen that medieval Europe was promiscuous, by any standards. Its sexual licence
was frequently riotous and therefore the impact of
syphilis certainly must, as described by Andreski,
have been tremendous. It was a sixteenth-century
AIDS, made even more terrifying by its completely
enigmatic nature. Tens of thousands of people were
turned overnight into rotting, walking corpses.
When syphilis colonies were built next to the
leper colonies in the cities, the lepers complained
about being put so close to such hideous-looking
and dangerous neighbours! Andreski admits the
great complexity of large historical changes, and
so syphilis can only be seen as one factor among
many, but he does make an ingenious argument
which is worth summarizing. It begins with the
relationship between syphilis and malaria.

In 1917 the Austrian doctor Wagner-Jauregg
began to treat syphilis patients in Vienna with doses
of malaria. He had discovered that the two diseases
were in some way mutually exclusive. We have
seen that the siege of Naples was the starting point
of the epidemic; but because malaria was prevalent
in most of southern Europe the disease became
more severe and more widespread the further north
it travelled. The reaction to the pox in northern
Europe, in other words, was different from the
reaction in the southern portion of the continent.
In the northern cities, a live-or-die law with respect
to sexual behaviour came into effect. Those who
practised continence, self-restraint, family loyalty

and marital fidelity survived; those who didn't, didn't. It is even suggested that the long-term disintegration of the European nobility was due at least in some measure to the ravages of a syphilis made possible by that class's stubborn promiscuity. At the court of Louis XIV, syphilitics were two a dozen. The most famous of them was the homosexual Duc de Vendôme, who suffered from a kind of anal chancre which came to be known as 'the crystallines' because they shone 'like crystals', as the doctor Ranchin observed. Saint-Simon was utterly disgusted by the sight of this diseased aristocratic lump, whose hands and feet, he wrote, 'were nothing but flaccid flesh which wobbled in every direction'; the face, with 'the appearance of an idiot', only increased his nausea. It is thought that the habit of wearing elaborate wigs and powder masks among the nobility, as well as smothering themselves in heavy perfume, came from their need to hide the ghastly track-marks of ravaging syphilis. Not so the merchants.

The fortunes of the two classes had been so far reversed by the middle of the eighteenth century that when the young Marquis de Sade, a blue-blood but bankrupt, first visited the palace of the banker whose daughter he was trying to marry, he was stunned by the grandeur and opulence of the bourgeois family house. But the bourgeoisie believed in and practised industry, morality and discretion; their aristocrat son-in-law did not. In the end, the promiscuous Sade and the prudent mother-in-law became deadly enemies, while the decline of the Marquis into an impoverished inmate of a madhouse organizing a theatre of lunatics in his spare time seems to ape the general fortune of his class.

The rise of the bourgeoisie was made possible by their continence. They practised a kind of sexual sanitation that was controlled not by the state, but by the family. Calvinism was the religion of the merchant, and this stern ethic didn't just repress sexual desire, it demanded an 'inner-worldly asceticism'. This asceticism led to the idealization of parsimony and was one of the factors which created the extraordinary economic dynamism of northern Europe in the puritan age.

Yet repression is not just a matter of inner-worldly asceticism; ritual purity, for example, the 'cleanliness' yearned for in the Old Testament, is as universal as the wheel.

Lepers were massacred *en masse* in China as late as the 1930s. The Hindu law-giver Yagnavalkya, in the third century AD, declared that leprosy was a moral not a physical disease: 'If one steals, he will get white leprosy.' In Indo-China it was lawful to murder lepers within city walls. They were buried alive in Sumatra, and in Tibet they were the object of a caste system which turned them into untouchables. Among the Zande of the Upper Nile, leprosy was even regarded as the fruit of incest.

A society yearns to be pure, clean and homogeneous. It is prepared to kill to get its way. In most cases, the racial stock is seen to be menaced by those internal 'outsiders' whose imaginary crimes have turned them into a contagion. In China, a leper's descendants were forbidden to marry until the fourth generation, to ensure that they would not breed. And in a German translation of the Talmud of 1762 it is declared that a Jew with leprosy may be 'unclean', but not a Gentile! The reasoning behind this subtle inversion is that only a Jew can be pure in the first place, and therefore only he can be made impure by disease. What has gripped the scribe is the importance of Levitical purity, the purity of the race . . .

In Christianity, however, the immemorial and universal notion of racial purity became fused with sexual pessimism. And from this completely improbable and malicious scenario, we can turn logically, if nightmarishly, to the Jew.

6
The Jew

Nothing causes the modern European more unease than the Jew. Before the Holocaust the Jew was the last in a long line of great polluters, distant descendant of the witch, the leper and the Moor. Because he had lasted longer as a type, he became more subtle, more complex and more interesting. In short, he became a kind of tubercular, the bearer of a tormented but intriguing pathology.

Nineteenth-century psychiatry was certainly convinced that Jews were sexually strange. Is Proust's Swann a typical sexual Jew? He chases after Odette, who has begun to deceive him, spies on her back door, visits her in the middle of the night in the hope of finding a naked cheater shivering in a corner. And in the end, although at first his behaviour seems to be that of any normal, jealous, man, he is branded by the excesses of a passion which has become improbable, exaggerated and *embarrassing*. He is left empty-handed, too: an immaculate outcast in his spotless white gloves and buttonhole. Is he afflicted with a Jewish pathology, though, that unique neurasthenia and obsessiveness fashionably ascribed to the Semite? By the time of the writing of *A la recherche du temps perdu*, the type had been well established, and, more than that, generally diffused in the air. The illustrious members of the Parisian Anthropological Society in the 1880s had pronounced neurasthenia to be a clinical condition of the Jew, and Charcot, in his *Tuesday Lesson* of 23 October 1888, set the seal on their deliberations. The Prussian census of 1880 had provided the starting point for a complete psychopathological portrait of this peculiar race, made up of the following characteristics:

1 Jews tend towards insanity. Krafft-Ebing wrote: 'Statistics have been collected with great care to show the percentage of insanity in various sects, and it has been shown that among the Jews the percentage is decidedly higher.' (*Textbook of Insanity*)
2 Jews tend towards sexual frustration and excessive sensuality because of religious hindrances to early and endogamous marriages.
3 Jews tend towards neurasthenia: 'nervous illnesses of all types are innumerably more frequent among Jews than among other groups.' (Charcot, *Tuesday Lesson*)
4 Jews suffer from the above through a lack of agricultural employment and an excess of cosmopolitanism.

5 Jews also suffer from 1 and 2 because of mystic fanaticism, or vice versa: 'Very often, excessive religious inclination is itself a symptom of an originally abnormal character or actual disease and, not infrequently, concealed under a veil of religious enthusiasm there is abnormally intensified sensuality and sexual excitement that lead to sexual errors that are of an aetiological significance.' (Krafft-Ebing, *Textbook of Insanity*)

Krafft-Ebing went on to create a startling portrait of the modern Jewish man in his study of neurasthenia. Sander Gilman, in his book *Jewish Self-hatred*, has shown how the neurasthenic, the capitalist and the urbanite usurer all merged in Krafft-Ebing's picture of the Jew. The Jew, in the first place, embodies the American axiom 'Time is money'. The Jew is even the quintessential American. He is 'an over-achiever in the field of commerce'. He spends his life 'reading reports, business correspondence, stock market notations during meals . . .'. This prejudice is reproduced even in Jewish writers. A noted Zionist like Martin Eglander could write that Jewish neurasthenia was the result of 'over exertion and exhaustion of the brain . . . [of the] struggle, haste and drive, the hunt for happiness' which we idly associate with capitalist culture.

By the turn of the century, then, the Jew had become a new tubercular: neurasthenic and over-refined. But unlike Gautier's ideal coughing, ninety-nine pound poet, the Jew didn't carry within him a desirable disease. On the contrary. His disease needed a cure.

The Jewess, by contrast, preserved her robust voluptuosity. In Stefan Zweig's 'The Burning Secret' the wife of a Jewish Viennese lawyer seduced by a young nobleman at the spa-town of Semmering comes under his eye in the company of her young son:

> She was, moreover, a type he liked very much: one of those slightly voluptuous Jewesses, in age not quite past her prime, clearly still capable of passion, but on the other hand experienced enough to conceal her inclinations behind an air of refined melancholy.

Refined melancholy now seems to be the mark of the Jew, and the Jewess easily becomes an odalisque, generously proportioned, sensual and enigmatically oriental – with an oriental melancholy to match.

But from this racial melancholia to the anguish of the self-hater is the shortest of steps. And what is most confusing about anti-Semiticism is that some of its most intellectually impressive proponents were themselves Jews.

Jewish writers often spoke of their mental 'disease' as if from personal experience. Such was the case with the renowned Jewish anti-Semite Arthur

Trebisch, who published his major work *Spirit and Judaism* in 1919. Just after publishing it, he suffered a sudden, and alarming, paranoiac delusion. Convinced that, because he had renounced his Jewish identity, he was being hounded by an '*alliance Israélite*', he fled through the streets of Berlin seeking refuge in different houses and feeling that he was being pierced by electromagnetic rays, which the fearsome *alliance* of bearded Yids was beaming into him as punishment. His notion of a world conspiracy was truly all-absorbing, and of course appealing to the young Nazis of the 1920s. The fact that it came from a Jew made it irrefutable.

In the same way, Trebisch's conviction that the pathology of the Jew impelled him to lie and misuse language made the latter identical in essence to that other mistress of the slippery tongue, woman. He was convinced that Jews had what he called a 'secondary perception' of the world, a lack of centre, created by their eternal waiting for a Messiah who would solve all the problems of history. This made them both rootless and degenerate. It also, needless to say, made them *mechanical* in their sex lives – for they were unable to have direct relationships of real love. The Jew, therefore, was the inventor of homosexuality and onanism. And with this rootless sexuality went an equally perverse wit: he was both joker and invert. The two went together.

Is this why the new 'Jewish language', psychoanalysis, was so obsessed with jokes, language and sex? Trebisch thought so, and for this reason was convinced that psychoanalysis could never cure non-Jews, with their more rounded, more complex personalities, and non-devious sexuality. Freud himself shared with Trebisch an interest in another Jewish Viennese thinker of this time, Otto Weininger, who in 1903 published a strange work called *Sex and Character*. Like Trebisch, Weininger was a self-hating Jew, and a few months after the publication of his book he committed suicide. He chose to do this in the room in which Beethoven had died, as if assimilating himself at the last moment with the very embodiment of the 'German Spirit'. But Weininger's anti-Semiticism was even stranger in that he could not separate the essences of Jews and females at all. For him, Judaism was not even simply a racial identity: it was a mental disease to which anyone could succumb!

What was the nature of this mental disorder? For Walter Rathenau, another Viennese intellectual, the Jew was feminine: the Jewish male was effete, and therefore quite alien. There is an old tradition linking women to irrational loquacity, persuasiveness and cunning. The Jew began to take on some of these characteristics. He was talkative, clever, a scribbler (like Heine, who invented German journalism), and above all manipulative. Jews and women shared a biology which made them misuse language by chattering and bandying nonsensical sophistries. This is an ancient conviction. In the Middle Ages, Christians were sometimes forbidden to talk to Jews in the streets for fear that their heads would be turned inside out. But by making the Jew female in character, the foxiness of the Semite was made yet more subtle. Now he was as treacherous as a woman, whose perfidy hardly had to be illustrated. And since a woman thought not by means of logic but by means of picturesque association, her Jewish replica could likewise be labelled 'logically insane'.

Even more obviously, the Jew could be made into a sexual predator. Women in the late nineteenth century were clearly predators – one need only recall the whey-faced vampires of Edvard Munch. And when the Jew, like woman, became a carrier of syphilis, as Hitler imagined, the circle closed. 'For hours on end,' Hitler wrote in *Mein Kampf*, 'with satanic joy in his face, the black-haired Jewish youth lies in wait for the unwitting girl whom he defiles with his blood, thus stealing her from her people . . . '

Whether the widespread rumour that Hitler's phobia had for its root a chance encounter with a Jewish whore in Vienna who left him with syphilis is true or not, the dream of the Jew as a predator of Aryan virgins, a kind of fairy-tale Wolf proficient in smooth-talking countless Red Riding Hoods, a virgin-stealer who *defiles with his blood*, has a surprisingly venerable history. All the ingredients in this nightmare were present from the beginning. From the beginning, the Jew was a smart talker; from the beginning, he was a goat in heat, with a whiff of leprosy about him. And from the beginning, need it be said, he also ate gold.

The sexual pessimism of the Christian has always been tied to his distrust of money. All of his moralisms, from the Middle Ages to the present day, have been directed against money and the place where it is made: the city. From the city sprang mercantile values, industry and the rupture with Nature. From the city, too, came moral disease. Not for nothing did Frank Lloyd Wright, talking of the cross-section of a city, compare it to the dissection of a malignant tumour. And who commanded this tumour if not the Jew?

When absolute feudalism began to lose its grip over Europe in the eleventh century and cities began to re-emerge, it was the Jew who pioneered its new money economy. The Church always treated usury as a mortal sin and maintained an elaborate system of charity: its values were incompatible with the urban economy, which it demonized by demonizing the Jew. It is incredible to think that this image was alive and well almost a millennium later. Indeed, it is still alive and well. The Jew is an exploiter; he is the Modern World incarnate. And of course he sums up in himself all of that world's barbarous sensuality.

The Jew who wears a top hat and who smokes a cigar, who controls the press and mass-markets pornography, represents nothing more nor less than our fraudulent hatred of our own wealth, sophistication and urbanism. How significant it is that one of the methods suggested by the Parisian psychologists to 'cure' the Jew of his malignant cosmopolitanism and lust was agricultural labour! For the Jew is the opposite of Nature; and wherever Nature is worshipped above modern life, Jews, or humankind in general, will be seen as a virus. What can be done with such a virus, other than to exterminate or control it? The mystic misanthropy is as sinister in the one as in the other. And the medieval Church is its ultimate source.

The persecution of heretics leading to actual executions began in the same century as the emergence of cities and of usurer Jews. The first heretics in history to be killed, Etienne and Lisois, were burned in 1022 in the town of Orléans, their trials surrounded by rumours of child murder and demonic orgies – just those aberrations which were to become so intimately connected with the Jew. Seventy-four years later, in 1096, the first pogrom took place when the Crusader Emicho of Leiningen went on a killing spree in the cities of the Rhine. The medieval Jewish chronicles of Solomon bar Simpson and of Rabbi Eliezer bar Nathan tell of the rampage of 'Count Emicho, the oppressor of the Jews – may his bones be ground to dust between iron millstones', in which a novel hatred of the Semite makes its début.

Guibert of Nogent, who chronicled these events from the Christian perspective, was fond of telling tales in his autobiographical *Monodiae* of 1115 of heresy and apostasy, in which the Jews aided blasphemous Christians to lose their souls. Sometimes they did this with an ample and scandalous libation of sperm. The Jew was thus unsubtly linked to the witch, though it seemed that from the very beginning of Christian history the Jew was a sorcerer: was it not a Jew who gave supernatural powers to the priest Theophilus in the Byzantine legend? At the end of the eleventh century, Paul of St Père of Chartres revived the legend of the Jewish sorcerer, claiming that the heretics burnt at Orléans had used powdered children's bones supplied by Levantines.

From the twelfth century on it was the mendicant friars who became the greatest enemies of the Jews. The friar Nicholas Lyra (1270–1349) launched into scathing analyses of Jewish sexuality, being in the first place scandalized by the vision of erotic frolics in the Heaven of the Talmud:

> Whence it is obvious that the Jews have fallen into the error of the Saracens, who define the beatitude of the future life as the corporeal delights of food and sex, which is deemed absurd not only among the Catholics, but also among the Gentile philosophers who view the beatitude of man in the works of his rational faculty. (*Postilla litteralis super Biblia*)

A widespread belief held that the Diaspora was the result of Adam's carnal mistake with Eve, though the Jews hotly disputed it. But the preachers lost no time in finding other scortatory scandals among the Chosen Race. Raymond Martini (1210–85), a Dominican from Barcelona charged with the censorship of Jewish books in Aragon, wrote perhaps the most savage pamphlet of his age in the *Puego fidei*, or *Dagger of the Faithful*.

Martini's argument flowed smoothly. The Devil had taken charge of the Jews and led them back to the Mosaic law, which was supposed to have been nullified by the Roman persecution (itself a sign that God was not pleased with the Chosen). The Jews were therefore heretical, irrational and lusty.

> Besides the spirit of fornication which is in their midst – that is, in their hearts – of whom ought it more appropriately to be said than of the devil Bentamalyon, that he restored to them circumcision, the Sabbath and other rituals which God removed through the agency of the Romans? The devil undoubtedly misled them and deprived them of a sense of understanding the truth, so that they are less intelligent than asses as regards divine scriptures.

When he runs up against the sexual frankness of the Talmud, he is even more upset. First, there was the story of Adam's copulating with Lilith and the demons, followed by the ridiculous suggestion that Noah had cursed Canaan after being raped or castrated by his son Ham. Even worse was the account of the orgy staged by Zimri ben Salu, for which he was done away with by Phinehas the priest (Num. 25) . . . or the sexual machismo of long-haired Samson: 'It is sufficiently obvious from these how fetid was the doctrine of the scribes – i.e. the teachers of the Jews – from the time that our Saviour came.'

But the most scandalous aspect of the Jews for Raymond, and perhaps the habit which best epitomized the depravity, was their custom of sucking the blood from the penis of a newly circumcised child. This seems to be the last straw for the preacher:

> Behold, reader, how God, in view of their crimes, placed the Jews in a terrible state of perception, so that they do what ought not to be done and is not becoming. And with what great guilt is that most abominable mouth, which quite often has blasphemed the Lord Jesus Christ, infected and punished! For as often as they circumcise an infant or an adult, they suck the penis orally for as long as blood emerges from it, desiring to obey the aforementioned mandate of the rabbis. They excuse this by saying that if this would not be done all their infants would die, which is false. For the Saracens circumcise their infants and never do this abominable act.

The goatishness of the Jew, his similarity to that strong-smelling and generally ardorous animal who seems to walk on two legs (as when rutting) and whose spooky horns remind us of those of a certain supernatural tyrant, who is modelled on him, was another aspect which no one sought to deny. Just like the Devil and goat, didn't the Jew have a funny little beard? And didn't he have a pungent smell, his *foetor judaicus*, which one could detect at a hundred yards? The Jew was thus a kind of perambulatory cheese, except that in his case there was nothing in the least appetizing about his bacteria. Later on, some prosaic pedants insisted that this smell derived from a habit of chewing garlic, but they missed its supernatural significance; for the smell of the Jew was the smell of his desire, the smell of the goat in heat.

One of the most outlandish characteristics of this shaggy creature, as Gilman showed, was that the male of the species actually *menstruated*. The thirteenth-century anatomist Thomas de Cantimpré wrote the first 'scientific' account of this bloody and improbable phenomenon, and supplied the sensational theory that it was a sign of the Father's curse by way of punishment for their denial of Christ. Like Eve, the Jew was marked by the stain of the Fall to an exceptional degree. A few hundred years later, Franco de Piacenza, in his list of Jewish 'maladies' of 1630, not only described the Jewish male as menstruating but as doing so a mere four times a year! It is only possible to imagine what precise image was running through Hitler's mind when he wrote of the Jew 'defiling with his blood'. Was he referring to the defilement of menstruation?

Such a creature was never going to get on well with Nature, and so for century after century doctors were unsurprised to find that Jews were on the whole more prone to illness than others. Grattenaur, in his *Concerning the Physical and Moral Characteristics of Contemporary Jews* (1791), mentioned quite specifically the 'whorishness and shamelessness' of the infected race, who fell ill so often because of their lascivious desires (not to mention a tendency to overspice their cooking). A year later, a medical survey of the Prussian provinces of Poland by La Fontaine came to the stirring conclusion that the greater incidence of sickness in the Jewish population, far from having anything to do with such mundane matters as sanitation or poor diet, was in reality the result of an unbridled appetite for love.

Was it the case, however, that these administrators and academics actually *saw* what they described? The Jew is actually a large imaginative complex, in which can be seen the leper, the sorcerer, the heretic and the libertine. And the same sexual pessimism which we have seen at work in Christian perceptions of these others was at work in him, with one difference: the Jew was also hated because he was rich.

The image of the Jew declined further in the nineteenth century, for a number of reasons. For Heine and for Nietzsche, the Greeks were superior to Jews because their culture was one of physical and psychological health. Heine even invented his famous categories of the Hellene and the Nazarene, the former being realistic, joyous and allied to life, the latter (Jews, Christianity) being ascetic, theoretical and iconoclastic. And whereas the sexuality of the former was radiant and naive, that of the latter was tortured by self-hatred.

This academic reaction against Judaism and its offshoots could not help finding itself debased by a merging with crueller, more folkish myths, medieval undercurrents which proposed a Jew who was not only excessively fond of incest but who was also a Shylock, a capitalist holed up in his fortified house who undermined the wholeness of the happy, primeval community.

In the Middle Ages, preachers like Peter Damiani, Valdes and Francis of Assisi upheld the psychological rule that for the rich man to enter Heaven he must go where camels cannot, through the eye of a needle. The distrust of money, planted so deeply, has never been uprooted. But money is of course the blood of civilization. And just as Jews were originally doctors, investors and advisors, a class of intellectuals and industrialists, they were the spleen which created this 'blood': they were civilization itself.

Now, it is well known that civilization has always been unpopular. It is little more than a hotchpotch of famous discontents. And an entire moral culture has been raised upon a gleeful disparagement of its oafish mistakes and arrogance. This apocalyptic counter-culture is essentially a culture of *nostalgia*, for it worships everything which the Jew is not: rootedness, the village, Nature, folk wisdom and what could be called the Forest. And have we not seen that sexual pessimism in all its forms also springs from nostalgia, from a nostalgia for the Garden of Eden? And what is the Jew if not the serpent who handed over the apple?

7

The Noble Savage

Because Eden was marked on maps it was always possible that one day, who knew when, someone would actually stumble on it. On 12 October 1492, it happened. Christopher Columbus landed on the island of Guanahani or San Salvador in the Caribbean and declared at once that the Garden of Eden had been found. The Isles of the Blessed had been discovered by modern navigation and the nautical technology of Iberia, and there seemed not the shadow of a doubt that the aborigines who lived there were the distant cousins of Adam and Eve, uncorrupted by the weight-driven clock.

Now, of course, Columbus is a villain. We have certainly accepted the proposition that the Americas were Eden, but we see its discoverer as the hand of disease. For Eden is a frail place and must be left alone. As soon as outsiders enter its gates, it falls apart. The Garden is a self-regulating ecology until the snake gets it into his head to innovate: *that* is where the trouble starts. Eden is like the Virgin:

once its ecological hymen has been pierced, it has lost its unique and splendid value.

What would have happened if Genghis Khan had arrived there first, or the fleet of Admiral Han which conquered Ceylon? Such questions never arise, partly because things have turned out the way they have and it is impossible to imagine them otherwise, but also because the European had a myth of Eden, which Genghis Khan didn't. And while the former felt guilt for his intrusion, the healthy Khan would have exterminated the Indians and then sent their ears in sacks to Karakoram without thinking about it twice.

Europe, however, is the culture which believes in the Noble Savage. When Bruce Chatwin, in his book on Australian aborigines, imagines Ibn Khaldun, the fourteenth-century Tunisian historian, gazing into the face of Genghis Khan, he is recalling the peaceful nomad, or those like Khaldun who sing his praises, confronting an old enemy, Settled Man. The latter is a warlike animal, given to demolishing his own cities, and never averse to the occasional genocide. Khaldun, like the Chatwin who sympathizes with him, was an urban intellectual who dreamt of being purged by the nomad. But what Khaldun admired in the nomad was his violence. Medieval Islamic states were in fact frequently taken over and revitalized by the very nomadic tribes who represented for Khaldun the austere, fluid values of the desert, closer to the heart of the Koran than the city. It is the softness and effeminacy of the city-dweller that Ibn Khaldun despises, his peacefulness. And what is it that Chatwin loves in the nomad? His immersion in the Garden? His lack of weapons? His immaculate purity? Or his putative lack of aggression?

He has charmingly forgotten *en route* that the cheerful Genghis lived all his life in a *tent*.

When Columbus set foot on Hispaniola, he was already prepared to meet a society of Eden-dwellers. The letters published by his son in Venice in 1571 show how unprepared he was for any kind of unpleasantness. The people were 'very gentle, not knowing what is evil, nor the sins of murder and theft'. He went on: 'They are a loving people, without covetousness . . . their speech is the sweetest and gentlest in the world, and always with a smile.'

A little later, Philip Amadas and Arthur Barlow, in their *First Voyage to the Coast of Virginia*, echoed these sentiments: 'We found the people most gentle, loving and faithful, void of all guile and reason, and such as live after the Golden Age.'

What is being described here is the world of Renaissance pastoral, with its bubbling brooks and happy shepherds. The descriptions are *literary*, however seriously they have always been taken. In a way, they remind one of the Japanese *Views of London* of the eighteenth century, which show the English capital as a bristling forest of pagodas, or the Dutch *Views of Benin*, which show the African city as a skyline of Dutch steeples. In Ralegh's *Discoverie of the Beautiful Empire of Guiana* we find the Noble Savage well developed on the banks of the Orinoco, smoking a pipe and philosophizing, like some wise extra-terrestrial from *Gulliver's Travels*, on the ways of the world. Needless to say, this leaves the Englishman gushing with admiration and reverence. The prototypes of Chactas, Chingachgook and Swift's Houyhnhnms are crystallizing.

The ground had long been prepared for the humanists, however. As far back as Antiquity the Roman historian Tacitus had enthused over the barbarians in *Germania*. The Germans were tough, democratic and hospitable. But what was especially significant about them was their chastity. Not for them the uproarious dinner parties and discreet sodomies of the contemptible Romans. Far from it. Rather like Ibn Khaldun's nomads, they were severe and incorruptible ascetics. And, of course, they never cheated, lied, swore, murdered or gambled. The Savage was an upright puritan, a Republican without the buckled shoes.

Rousseau and Montaigne were both moved by *Germania*, and adapted passages from it to their own uses. Montaigne was by far the most extravagant and doctrinaire propagandist of the Noble Savage, a type he cultivated with no trace of his customary scepticism. Two essays set out his adoration of the Savage: *Of the Cannibals* (Chapter XIII of Book I) and the lesser known *On Coaches*. *Of the Cannibals*, a delicious exercise in self-hating cultural relativism, invents a Utopia in standard literary fashion based on travellers' publications. We learn that the autochthons are not barbarous or inferior, but in fact 'internally' cultured and superior. Why are they superior? Because among them 'there is ever perfect religion, perfect policy and complete use of things'. The Caribs exude from every pore those 'profitable virtues which we have bastardized'. Montaigne adds: 'Plato and Lycurgus could not imagine a gentility so pure and simple . . . nor believe that our society might be maintained with so little art and humane combinations.'

Montaigne never tires of the term 'bastardize' to describe civilization, or, as we now have to rephrase it, 'civilization':

> But at least they are free from the manifold evils which accompany our civilization, and which make our vaunted progress a mockery. The whole verneer of our civilization had covered, stifled and misdirected a hundred natural activities comparable to the instinctive skill of the bird and the spider . . . Nature keeps them good and happy under her own laws which we, to our detriment, have *bastardized*. (My italics)

Montaigne here is a kind of dictionary of contemporary clichés. Under P, for example, we would find '*Progress*: mockery, outmoded religious dogma (now anachr.) *see* phlogiston'; under V we would find '*Verneer*: synonym for Civilization, *see* cosmetics'; under C, '*Civilization*: psychoanalytic concept, now disused, derived from colonial slang, *see* gunship, opium'; and finally, under S, '*Savage*: (anachr.) synonym for forest-dwelling Buddhist'.

The belief in spontaneous virtue reached heights of self-delusory absurdity very early on. The dramatist Aphra Behn claimed that the nations of Surinam, and therefore all primitive peoples, had no word for the concept of 'deceit', and would probably never even have listened to the report of the Jesuit linguist Pellepart, who provided no fewer than five synonyms used in Surinam for 'liar' alone. The Noble Savage was too seductive, and his magical properties made him untouchable.

The most powerful voice raised in defence of the New World Indians, and the direct progenitor of the fantasies of the scribes sitting in Europe in their ventilated studies, was the Spanish bishop Bartolome de Las Casas, whose *Brevisima relación de la destrucción de las Indias* appeared in 1542.

Las Casas was not a study-bound intellectual, however. Like all the Spanish writers on the American peoples, he had travelled and worked in the colonies. His publications were a passionate defence of indigenous innocence, directed at the studies which had painted a hostile picture of Indian mores. For Las Casas, the Indians were tender lambs before the wolves, lions and tigers, of the Conquest. Amid his indignant accusations of genocide and torture, he takes care to deal with the issue of sodomy, for the crusade against the native Americans had been undertaken in the name of three cardinal matters: cannibalism, drug-taking and sodomy.

Sodomy became the nucleus of the controversy which raged between Spanish clerics and administrators in their dealings with Indians. Las Casas had to deny the existence of sodomitic practices among the virginal creatures whose right to freedom he was defending. While reluctantly admitting sodomy among the Mayans, and attributing its popularity to the demon Cu, he categorically denied its indulgence in any other Mesoamerican society.

Las Casas was supported by the father of sixteenth-century Spanish theologians, Francisco de Victoria, acknowledged now as the founder of International Law. Victoria's condemnation, in 1537, of claims to dominion in the New World attacked the imperial argument which justified domination on the basis of a suppression of sodomy:

Fourth Conclusion: The Christian princes cannot wage war on the infidels on account of the sin against nature, that is, because of sodomy rather than on account of the sin of fornication. The conclusion is proved because the faithful do not have better dominion over the infidels than the infidels over the Christians. On the same grounds it should follow that the King of the French could make war on the Italians because they commit sins against nature (i.e. sodomy) . . .

To this was added a celebration of Indian chastity. Hernando Pizarro himself, in a book written in prison following his disgrace in 1533, describes the nunneries and virgin-worship of the Incas. And later, the Augustinian cleric Alonso Ramos Gavilan, in the *Historia del sanctuario de Na. Sa. de Copocobana*, printed at Lima in 1621, described the chastity vows undertaken by Inca women in the service of the Sun God. Of the 120-year-old virgin of Uracha he wrote: 'she had been dedicated to the Sun, and for that reason no Indian dared to have evil relations with her.'

One of the more magisterial accounts of Indian life is the *Monarchia indiana*, printed at Seville in 1615 by the Franciscan friar Juan de Torquemada, a reliable and sober work containing a long dissertation on sodomy which compares the enjoyment of anal delights in the ancient world with the same practice among the Mayana of Veracruz in Guatemala:

Some in those provinces were found with the nefarious sin [sodomy] and thus there was a law that prohibited it because, although it is true that they did not always use this bestial vice, in the end this corruption was introduced into the republics in the following way. There appeared to them a devil under the figure of a young man who was named Chin . . . and he induced them to commit it with another demon in his presence, and from that there came many among them who said it was not a sin.

Convinced therefore that it was not a sin, the custom started among parents of giving a boy to their young son, to have him for a woman and use him as a woman; from that also began the law that if anyone approached the boy they were ordered to pay for it, punishing them with the same penalties as those breaking the condition of marriage . . .

But while Torquemada followed the example of Las Casas (the demons Chin and Cu are of course the same), general division over the angelic condition of the Indians could not have been more intense. Even the initial impressions of the first navigators offered no harmony, for Amerigo Vespucci contradicted Columbus on every point. Having accompanied Alonso de Ojeda's exploration of the Amazon and the Magdalena river in 1499, and accomplished an expedition for the Portuguese in 1501 which took him to Margarita Island, Vespucci wrote a letter to Piero Soderini in 1504 concerning the latter. 'In looks and behaviour,' he wrote, 'they were very repulsive and each had his cheeks bulging with a certain green herb which they chewed like cattle so that they could hardly speak . . .' This is the first description in history of cocaine abuse, the 'herb' being ground, calcinated shells mixed with coca leaves.

The cipher for most of the first-hand reports from the voyages of Magellan and Columbus was Pietro d'Anghiera, whose *Decales* of 1516 contains one of the earliest hostile accounts of Indian sodomy. Writing of Nuñéz de Balboa's expedition of 1513 to Querera in Panama, d'Anghiera noted (I use here Eden's translation of 1555): 'Vasco found the house of the Kynge infected with the most abhominal and unnaturall lechery. For he found the Kynge's brother and many younger men in womans apparell, smoth and effeminately decked which he abused with preposterous Venus.'

D'Anghiera also reported, however, that the Indians detested homosexuality, punished it severely and were convinced that it lay at the root of national disorders. Columbus's physician on the second expedition of 1493, Diego Chanca, also described homosexual customs on the island of Turupueria (Guadeloupe):

> To the boys made captive, they cut off the members and use them until they become men, and then when they wish to make a feast they kill them and eat them, for they say that the flesh of boys and women is not good to eat. Of these boys, three came fleeing to us with their virile members cut off . . .

The Spaniards were clearly fascinated by this Indian

vice, which so closely resembled their own, and occasionally their revulsion got the better of them. Hence the fulminating friar Tomas Ortiz gave testimony in 1525, upon which authority the Caribs were declared slaves and the three accusations of anthropophagy, drug addiction and sodomy were first made official. 'They were donkeys,' he wrote, 'dumb, crazy and without sense . . . They were cowards like hares, dirty little pigs, ate lice, spiders and raw worms.' Given their dietary habits, their sexual proclivities went without saying.

The more serious Spanish anthropologists were much more curious than Ortiz and his ilk. One such dispassionate observer was Gonzales de Orvieto, who published a perceptive work called *Historia general de las Indias* in 1535. This book contains much of the experience which Gonzales gleaned from his years as Supervisor of Gold Smelting, beginning with the expedition of Pedrarias Davils in 1514. His wide-ranging descriptions of homicide, suicide, cannibalism, sodomy, incest and drug-taking could only enrage Las Casas, but the latter was not able to demonstrate in his own texts a greater familiarity with these societies than the Supervisor of Gold Smelting.

On sodomy, Gonzales wrote that, 'as soon as they fall into this guilt, they wear *naguas* skirts like women and they wear strings of beads and bracelets'. He says that 'they are extremely hated by the women' and that the word *camoyoa* (homosexual) was a frequent term of abuse. Gonzales also left an interesting account of a series of pornographic gold tablets depicting images of sodomy, which he was ordered to destroy in Darién. Overall, his conclusion is that sodomy was practised widely in the Indian ruling classes, that homosexual brothels existed in most cities, and that suppression of homosexuality in the lower classes was ruthless.

The Spanish themselves had a whole lexicon to describe the practice. The most commonly used terms were of course *sodometico* and *sodomia*, but in addition to these there were *vicio nefando* (hidden vice), *pecado abominable* (abominable sin) and *contra natura*. The word *bardaje* from the Arabic *bardach* and Persian *bardah* (a captive young man) was popular. The youth submitting to sodomy was called a *mancebo* (from the Latin *mancipium*, or slave) and the practice itself *mancebia*. More colloquially, they are *amarianados*, from Mary, which is to say, effeminates.

That the Spanish had such a developed vocabulary shows how intense was their interest in investigating what they called the *inhonesto vicio*, but also how important it was to their overall pessimism regarding the Indians. The Nahuatl-speaking historian Motolinia wrote darkly of the frenzy let loose during the Panquezaliztli festival, with its ritual burnings, human sacrifices and anthropophagy: 'This land was a transfer to Hell, to see the inhabitants at night shouting, some calling the devils, others drunk, others singing and dancing.' The Bacchants were reduced to the level of 'animal brutes' under

the effect of teuanacatlh mushrooms, the taking
of which frequently led to murder. And the
even-handed chronicler Bernadino de Sahagún,
the father of Mexican anthropology, in the *Historia
general de las cosas de Nueva España*, has left a litany
of unsensational accounts of ceremonial infanticide,
flaying, burnings and eating of slaves (in a meal
called *tlacatloalli*), as well as death sentences for
virtually every infringement of the moral code,
including the drinking of alcoholic *pulque*, and the
public execution of homosexuals.

Sahagún wrote at least one version of the *Historia*
in Nahuatl and was widely travelled in Central
America. But doubts about the Indians extended
far beyond the competence of neutral observers,
to a point where the papacy itself could not decide
whether the Indians were 'rational' or not. It was
not until 1537 and the two Bulls *Sublimis Deus* and
Veritas ipsa that Indian rationality was conceded,
and even then the Bulls had to be hastily withdrawn
in 1539 when it was found that they were in conflict
with the *Intera cetera* of 1493, which had given
power over the Indian populations to the Spanish
Crown. The papacy wavered; two versions of the
Indian – angel and demon – fought a pitched battle
in the Castilian publishing houses, and the Garden
of Eden teetered in the balance.

It is customary now to accuse the Spanish of bias,
but that bias leaned two ways at the same time. The
unreliability of Las Casas is obvious in the light of
Indian texts themselves; the rhetoric of Ortiz howls

too loud in the opposing corner. If Ramon Pane in his text of 1496 was the first man in history to describe syphilitic ulcers, then the commentary of Orvieto is never far behind him: 'See how just it is what God gave the Indian where such a thing is done . . .'

Europeans wanted an Indian different from themselves. The Noble Savage or the Debased Savage are expressions of his equally virulent self-hatred and self-certainty. What they never bargained for, what in any case no culture would have bargained for, was the possibility that the savage was neither noble nor debased, but, in eerily unexpected ways, exactly like themselves.

The Mexican anthropologist Francisco Guerra has collected the surviving Indian codices in his study of pre-Columbian sexual aberration, and in them we see a society whose repression of what it saw as sexual crime was almost indistinguishable from that of its conquerors. Most of the Indian cultures, that is to say, practised confession, penance, self-mutilation, public humiliation and *autos-da-fé*. Most sorts of 'deviants' were summarily put to death.

The historian Mendieta, writing in 1596, had observed that adulterers in the Aztec cities, for example, were 'killed tied hand and foot', their heads pounded with stones until they were 'left like cakes'. Sahagún, translating directly from a Nahuatl text, gave some idea of the Aztec detestation of homosexuality: 'The sodomite is an effeminate, a defilement, a corruption, a filth; a taster of filth, revolting, perverse, full of affliction. He deserves laughter . . . he is nauseating . . . He makes one acutely sick . . . he merits being committed to flames.' In his *Apologetica historia* he chronicles the custom of killing incestuous fathers with their daughters by strangulation, and likewise incestuous brothers and sisters, and lesbians.

The most striking Indian book on sexual punishments is that of Alva Ixtlilxochitl (1570–1649), a descendant of the Alcolhua kings of Texcoco, a province of which he governed under the Spanish. In the early 1600s he assembled a large library of pre-Columbian documents which survives today in the Jesuits' library in Mexico City. As a cipher for Indian chroniclers, he is of unique importance, and his codex of 1605, written in Nahuatl, contains the fullest account of the sexual penal system of ancient Mexico. His reciting of a series of laws called the Ordinances of Nezchualcoyotzin is worth quoting at some length:

> 1st. That any woman who committed adultery to her husband, if seen by the husband, she and the adulterer to be stoned to death in the market.
>
> 2nd. That any person who forced anybody (committed sodomy) and sold him as a slave to be hanged.
>
> 7th. That any daughter of any lord or knight found bad, to die for it . . .

13th. That anyone found sodomitic, to die for it . . .

14th. That any man or woman who acted as a procurer of married women to die for it . . .

The nefarious sin, sodomy, was punished in two ways. To the one acting as the female, they removed his entrails from the bottom, he was tied down to a log and the boys from the town covered him with ash until he was buried; and then they put a lot of wood and burnt him. The one acting as the male was covered with ash and tied down to a log until he died . . .

The adulterer was killed by crushing his head between two stones.

Ixtlilxochitl then translates this prophecy from the mid-fifteenth century:

In a year like this [1467] this temple of Nuitzilopochtli will be destroyed . . . the evil, pleasures and lewdness will reach their summit and men and women will give themselves to lust from their tender years. To save our children from these vices and misfortunes you should lead them from childhood into work and virtue.

Couldn't these same sentiments have been taken directly from an edifying mural in a nineteenth-century workhouse? But even greater confusion lies in wait where the revision of the Savage has recently denied the charge of both cannibalism and of internal repression. Unfortunately, the Indian texts themselves, when they adopt an indignant tone against the arrogance of the Spanish, actively boast of the repression of 'deviants' by violence. The greatest of the Indian historians writing in Spanish was Garcillasso de la Vega, whose *Commentarios reales de los Incas* depicts in detail the suppression by successive Incas of tribes associated with homosexuality. Garcillasso himself was a descendant of the Inca royal family, and his accounts seem to be a proud assertion of the Incas' moral severity when it came to the wretched inverts.

The general Auqui Titu, for example, was ordered by the Incas to burn homosexuals alive in the marketplaces. Their houses were then burnt, the trees in their land uprooted to extirpate even their memory, and the whole town terrorized for its own salvation: 'and it would be proclaimed as an inviolable law, because the sin of an individual would destroy the whole town and would burn all the inhabitants'.

Among the Huayllas, a mountain people, the suppression of catams by the Inca Capac Yupanqui took similar forms of public terror, with executions by burning and destruction of property. Garcillasso even informs us that the very word denoting a homosexual was almost unspeakable among the Incas, and when used as an insult would lead to homicidal violence.

Several other Indian writers confirmed the cruelties of the penal code in their own societies.

The Tlaxcaltec Diego Muñoz Camargo wrote in 1576: 'They [the Tlaxcaltecs] considered a great abomination the nefarious sin, and the sodomites were despised and considered very low, and treated like women . . .'

Camargo described human sacrifices among the Tlaxcaltecs as well, placing them within a cycle of confession, self-mutilation and catharsis. Gaspar Antonio Chi, a Mayan, and son of the famous Mayan priest Napuc Chi, described the prisons 'in which they put children condemned to death and for sacrifice'. Chi made it clear that there was only one punishment for even the most trivial transgression, and that was instant death. And two Inca writers, Huaman Poma de Ayala (1615) and Blas Valera (1590), portrayed the public burnings of prostitutes, homosexuals, lesbians, heretics and adulterers. Poma tells of the 'punishment of lewd virgins by hanging them from their hair'.

The illuminated codices also demolish the quaint picture of Indian culture erected by aficianados of the Noble Savage. The magnificent Codex Magliabecchi, dated to 1565, follows in pictographs the twenty Mexican-days and the fifty-two-year cycle, concentrating on certain festivals, in particular the sexual feast of Pillavanaliztli, which was devoted to drinking and the sexual initiation of children. The illustrations clearly show rituals of anthropophagy, with the division of the body into edible segments served with different vegetables. There are also curious pictures of the *temazcalli* steam baths, which acquired the same bad reputation as their European counterparts. We see medical divination by maize grains, one reading of which indicates a connection between sodomy and sickness. Numerous depictions of penance and medical confessions recall medieval Spanish woodcuts showing exactly the same thing. For as in Europe, this classification of sexual sin, its punishment and atonement, rested upon the act of confession.

In 1617, the General Inspector of Idolatries under the Archbishop of Lima, Fernando de Avenado, wrote an intelligent and sensitive report on Indian customs which includes accounts of these ritual confessions, which recall in every way the auricular confession, or *exhomologesis*, of the Catholics. On 3 April of that year he wrote the following to his prelate D. Bartolomé Lobo Guerra:

> The Incas confess of their theft, of having more than one woman, of killing other people, and at the end of their confession, the priest told them to mend their ways and commit themselves truly to the *huacas*, and gave them the little stone with the powders to blow them off and offer them to the Sun or the *huacas*; and in other provinces they wash in the river, assuming the water washed away their sins. At the end of their confessions they offered rabbits called *coy* and the sheep of the country. After the sacrifices they begin fasting.

The parallels with early Christianity are extra-ordinary.

Another historian interested in Indian confession was Antonio de Remesal. In his history of Chiapa and Guatemala of 1617 he wrote:

In many parts of New Spain was found the confessions of sins. Those of Tlaxaca professed vocal confession of the guilt they had . . . it was the way of confessing the Spaniards found in the province of Nicaragua. They told their sins in secret to a priest who could not reveal them. In Yucatan was also found the confession of sin. The jurisdiction of this confession did not reach the sins of the mind, but were only concerned with acts, thefts and all sorts of sexual crimes. Those women in childbirth and parturition were confessed by other women . . .

After confession, the faithful were flogged with nettles, often by designated cripples or people suffering other deformities such as hunchbacks: in Cuzco there was a whole caste of these hunchbacks who whipped the penitent. The confessions might involve whole populations attempting to expiate sins on a national level after an earthquake . . . or more intimate curing of diseases of the mind or the exorcism of lustful demons. For yet again, the Indians echoed Europeans in their belief that sexual crimes could be the effect of an incubus or an evil spirit. We know that the Mayans used incantations as a form of medicine, because such cures for sexual promiscuity have survived in a manuscript called the Codex of the Bacabs – the Bacabs being the four major Mayan gods.

The Mayan doctor regarded himself as being able to effect a mental disorder by influencing the *ik*, or 'wind', which entered the patient and made him, or her, excessively passionate. Astrological symbols, or *muts*, were assigned to each patient and to plants related to them. The incantor made reference to these as he effected his cure.

The language of the Bacabs book is esoteric and mystic, but the hostility to erotic pleasure is not mysterious at all:

> The words for the erotic-seizure. Mad will be the speech of the man because of the fever. The man has an impulse to run because of his fever . . . High is the door of the green arbour, where the origin of the lust of their birth, the lust of creation took place. I curse you, dwarf-man wind, together with erotic seizure.

The text then runs on: 'This would be recited over the man who talks very madly. He runs afflicted with a convulsion. This shall be twice recited over him, twice repeated.'

How does this describe the sexuality of the Indian? Gone at least is the chaste warrior of Rousseau singing his virtuous bird-song like a kind of human nightingale. Gone for that matter is the simple and sexless lamb of Montaigne. The invader had wanted a being whose sexuality contained no conflict; but almost without noticing it, he found one whose torment was as familiar as his own face. We can put this another way. As the Europeans emerged from the Middle Ages they craved for proof that biblical innocence could be refound, and the infernal logic of the Fall evaded. Isn't this what all nostalgia for the Garden comes to? But because the Indian was merely a vehicle for this nostalgia – *as he still is* – his own sexual pessimism was lost. Las Casas invented the Spanish 'genocide' in the Antilles in the text of 1542 – an inaccuracy which enraged his contemporaries, who knew that smallpox had decimated the islands – because what he wanted was a resurrection of Eden, and Eden could not have anything in it but *victims*. Who wants to remember that the ball games played in the superb courts of Monte Alban often ended with the disembowelling of the losing side? The real pessimism of the Indians, which makes their culture so unusual, has been lost on the way.

Diego Rivera painted panoramas of Aztec cities splendid with a system of Indian socialist welfare, a sort of ancient Bolshevik Russia without the steam trains. But the heart of this disappeared world really lies elsewhere. In the figures of Death being masturbated by castrated eunuchs and women, in the sodomitic drinking vessels of the Peruvian Mochica and Chimu, with their obscene spouts and apertures, in the images of forest animals copulating with this same Death, whose shadow falls over everything in an art which expresses, as Guerra puts it, 'the practice of every possible sexual aberration to an extent never recorded in the history of civilization'. And we see it reborn in the stark woodcuts of Huaman Poma's text, which foreshadow the sombre violence of the revolutionary Mexican artist Posada, with their scenes of epilepsy, revel and pessimistic cruelty.

In these images of an 'alien heart', there is nothing we do not immediately and instinctively understand.

8
Don Juan

If the Noble Savage was the sixteenth century's most unconvincing invention, its most ridiculous was Don Juan. Like the Savage, however, Don Juan was disposed to music, and in the end carved out a blameless operatic career for himself.

Gendarme de Bavotte, the industrious scholar of Don Juan arcana, claimed that his subject was the only myth which Europe in its entirety accepted as its own. Not only did the fantastical Don know a continental success, but he also became a specimen, which medicine occasionally stooped to examine with a certain amount of bemused reverence. What fascinated doctors was the terrible possibility that Don Juan might actually be real. Was he a male *type*, which could be cured with drugs? Did he have pathological characteristics, like epileptics, witches and Jews? Or was he a biological entity with its own physical quirks, an individual of whom it could be said

– just as one might describe a body as being a mesomorph or an ectomorph – that he was a *DonJuanomorph*?

The literary explanations for Don Juan are so boring that one can hardly stay awake reading them. Why do writers have so much trouble with him? Could it be that Don Juan is in fact now utterly incomprehensible? One of the more interesting accounts of Don Juan was written in 1813 by E.T.A. Hoffmann and is called *Don Juan: A fantastic event which befell a travelling enthusiast.* It is not one of Hoffmann's more poetic tales, being made up almost entirely of theory. The first part of the story, however, is quite effective. A traveller stops at a provincial hotel one night. As he is sitting in his room he hears an orchestra tuning up nearby and discovers that a performance of Mozart's opera *Don Giovanni* is being planned for that evening. Delighted, the amateur opera lover procures his seat. That night, in his box, he discovers to his astonishment that he is sitting next to Donna Anna – that is, to the actress who plays Donna Anna. Later that night, he writes a long letter to her explaining his version of Mozart's work (a pedantic kind of love letter to write to a woman you have just met – she would almost certainly have thrown it in the fire in disgust). As he is writing, he suddenly smells her perfume near him, and the following morning discovers that she died during the night, the whiff of scent having romantically coincided with her death. This first scene can be seen as a kind of spooky envelope which contains the letter itself, a long discursion on Don Juan. And what Hoffmann has to say is this: that Da Ponte and Mozart do not tell the same story. The writer wonders why, after all, Don Juan is so important. Why does he receive a supernatural punishment? The form of the story says nothing. It is the music which opens up the Don's soul. And the Don, above all, is a yearner for transcendence. His myth has in fact survived from a much earlier, more primitive, age, and by the year 1813 it had already lost its meaning. A century later the novelist Artur Brausewetter, in his *Don Juans Erlösung*, summed up Hoffmann's scepticism: 'Mozart created this tragedy in immortal sounds, but its poet is yet to come.'

The psychoanalyst Otto Rank for one was not taken in by the search of the 'medicalists', as he called them, for a real Don Juan, nor by the transcendent readings of Hoffmann and, later, Kierkegaard. 'The easy conqueror of woman,' he stated baldly, 'so familiar to popular consciousness through its tradition, has in fact never existed. Consequently we can conclude that the essence of the Don Juan material is more profound than the frivolous breaking of hearts; rather, that from the beginning the legend and drama must have sought and found something else.'

But the Freudian reading that follows doesn't

seem any more satisfactory, because the individual *ticks* of the legend, its specific eccentricities, are not really made intelligible. You are always aware of the psychoanalytic machinery grinding away in the background. It is also, on a vulgar level, disappointing to see literalism so haughtily and brutally dismissed. It is equally disappointing to be told by Max Frisch, in the *Don Juan* of 1952, that the Don is exciting to women because he prizes something more than women – possibly even atomic physics. One feels like walking out of the room in disgust. Why must the Don always be 'read' as if he were a piece of coded jargon which can be deciphered into plain, sensible sentences or turned into a quivering bundle of innocuous metaphysical speculations – as if he were a superman not of the boudoir but of the seminary? It is difficult not to feel a growing sympathy with those white-moustached nineteenth-century Spanish doctors who frantically searched for 'proof' that Don Juan was not a pasty arty metaphor but an animal as real as a hedgehog or a desert rat. Their whole outlook is infinitely more naive, but also, *if it turned out to be true*, infinitely more fascinating. For the most interesting thing that we can imagine about Don Juan is that he was in fact rooted in history.

What, for instance, if the Romantics were right and Don Juan was Don Miguel de Mañara, the repentant libertine who in old age became Brother

Superior of the Spanish Brothers of Charity? Juan de Cardenas wrote his spurious biography, full of insalubrious incidents which we are now invited to despise. But the Mañara stories are truly Don Juanesque. The story of the rape in the church, for example. Mañara goes into a church in pursuit of a woman and, relentlessly pestering her, finally drags her into an embrace. She resists, he insists. After a messy struggle, she gives in and takes off her veil. Surprise, surprise: a female skeleton! This is a late version of an ancient morality tale told in the Majorcan story of the fourteenth-century Catalan mystic Raimondo Lullio, who also pursued a woman into a church, to be confronted with a naked breast eaten away with cancer: the shock provoked his conversion to chastity. In another Mañara story, the seducer goes to his lover's room and, instead of the delectable conquest he has been waiting for, finds a corpse spread out on the bed, so causing him to waver in a moment of uncertain and tasteless necrophilia.

The Mañara legends appealed to the Romantics. Mérimée's Don Juan in *Ames du purgatoire* is based on them, as is Dumas' *Juan de Manara*. But what excited the Romantics was the certainty that Mañara had actually existed. The Don was a type which lay hidden under the surface of everyday life, and he was at least as dangerous as the Frankenstein which science was one day going to build.

What did the doctors say? Here is Dr Gregorio Marañon, who in an earlier pamphlet, *Notas para la biología de Don Juan*, had declared emphatically that 'hyper-genitality' was not a feature of the indefatigable lover:*

The morphology of the man endowed with an extraordinary capacity for sexual love is, in general, inaesthetic; smallish stature, short legs, a face with somewhat pronounced features, rough skin with a lot of hair, large beard. They do not resemble in the least the Don Juan whom we see gliding across salons and theatre stages: svelte, elegant, with fine skin, supple, curly hair, with a slender moustache and a little, pointy beard. The laboured appearance of this latter type, and sometimes his eccentricity, only heightens still more his absence of virility.

So Dons are ugly, puny, hairy, with ballooning beards and unheroic genitalia. It was always possible that their excessive desire was linked to a malfunction of the pituitary gland. On the other hand, this same doctor has much to say on the mystic roots of Don Juanism: 'An eroticism deformed into a delirium,' he writes, 'was in effect one of the most frequently recurring elements in the collective psychological state of early seventeenth-century

* In French, *Don Juan et le don juanisme*, trans. Marie-Berthe Lacombe (1958).

Spain.' Marañon is referring to the heretical sect called the Illuminatos, which was found guilty of sexual profanities under the reign of Philip IV. But if the Don is a Spanish perversion, with a typically Spanish desire to desecrate the holy, his story, the legend's form, is a Dark Ages folk-tale which can be found all over Europe.

Tirso de Molina's *El burlador de Sevilla*, published in 1630, was the first full Don Juan to appear, but by then Don Juan was already long familiar. We see him in the nineteenth-century character of Don Felix Montenar in José Espronceda's *El estudiante de Salamanca*. Over the centuries, he underwent several transformations: a *commedia dell'arte* seducer in the *Il convitato di pietra* of Cicognini; the suave rogue of Villiers' and Dormion's *Festin de Pierre*; and finally Mozart's puzzle. But the form of his story remained the same. Don Juan insulted a dead man, who invited him to dinner (or vice versa), and as punishment he was dragged down into the Underworld. And this provocation of the Stone Man or the Dead Commander is the archaic, primitive part of the story, which is its key.

The folk-lore scholar Dorothy Mackay has compiled the sources of the Don Juan myth in European folk-tales, gathering together eighty-one 'invitation' stories from Iceland to Portugal. 'In popular European tradition,' she says:

there exists among the folklore of the dead a group of tales in which a living man, as he walks, comes upon a dead one, represented in a variety of physical forms, and invites the dead man to dine with him. The invitation, in itself an offence to the dead man, is frequently accompanied by some physical violence such as a kick or a tweak. The dead man, outraged by the affront, accepts the invitation and appears at his living host's dinner chiefly for the purpose of inviting him to turn up for a later time. When the living man keeps the rendez-vous of the second invitation – and keep it he must – he is forced to pay for his sins at the hands of the supernatural host, or is at least warned by him of the punishment to follow if he does not reform.

In most cases, the offender kicks the dead man's skull – probably reflecting the Christian importance accorded to the part of the body which is baptized. In the romances collected by Ramón Pidal in Segovia in the early 1900s, skull-kicking stories appear frequently. In *La laura mundi*, Leonti, one of the best-known pre-Don Juans, insults a skeleton and invites it home. When the phantomic remains turn up for dinner the insulter is dragged off to Hell, as Don Juan is. And another compiler, Alphonse de Cock, retells several skull-profanation stories, including one in which a pigeon-keeper waters his birds in a skull while a character called Orain tells the story of one Le Bédeau de Chanteloup, who played ball games with skulls and who was dragged away to the cemetery by phantoms during his wedding, only to be found decapitated the following day, his head in his hand like a football.

Why, then, is Don Juan saddled with a cumbersome story that doesn't fit, as Hoffmann said he was? Because he began life as a skull-kicker, not as a lover. Offending the dead is his crime, and that is a primitive taboo. These are pagan stories, dressed in Christian language. And since the dead are a radiant hierarchy which polices the land of the living, the swaggering skull-kicker who insults them can only expect the death sentence.

Medieval tales, however, are full of the titillating proximity of sex and the dead. Time and again, we meet people creeping into nunneries at night who unexpectedly meet processions of the dead, like those rumoured to roam around the countryside on All Souls' Day, the Day of the Dead. The price of such an encounter was always death by dawn. The Don Juan legend was born from a world in which pleasure and death had not failed to attract each other, for All Saints' Day was the elegant invention of Bishop Odilo of Cluny in 998. By making the pagan Roman feasts of the dead known as Ferulia and Lemuria coincide with a Christian feast, he hoped to tone down the sexual riots of the Roman death festivals still popular in the Catholic world. Prior to his act, this orgiastic outpouring had even taken place in churches on the Day of the Dead – to the extent that, in the year 893, Hincmar of Rheims had to forbid the clergy from drinking on that day. The dead not only forced the living to obey the supernatural laws of mortality, but also gave them a day's holiday in which to let themselves go, to commune with them through excess. The Christian and pagan relations to the dead grappled with each other throughout the Middle Ages, and it was not until 1541 that the lepurian festivities were outlawed by the synodal decree of Antonius of Guevarra, Archbishop of Montevideo. Don Juan, then, was born out of a world whose ambiguous relations with the dead had not been resolved. But for him at least the latter were *real* – more real than himself.

This is why Don Juan has disappeared. The dead themselves have disappeared as a force to be reckoned with. We no longer imagine ourselves surrounded by armies of hovering phantasmal corpses, ready like the deceased masses of the city of Rome in *Julius Caesar* to squeak and gibber in the streets when they return *en masse* to avenge their indignities. The Italian novelist Sandro Veronesi, in *Gli sforiati*, imagines the dead of Rome rising up on a national holiday and taking the bus to Ostia to see if the old place has changed at all. They have problems understanding the phrase *obliterare un biglietto* (after all, are they themselves '*obliterati*'?); they wander around feeling nostalgic, eat sandwiches at the beach, or try to, and go back to their graves for a nap. The dead today are a form of irony or they are nothing. And when we stopped believing in them, or rather, when we stopped fearing them, shame, purity, repentance, honour, tragedy, eschatological drama, at least the primitive form of sexual pessimism, and Don Juan, died.

9

The Oriental

If Don Juan had ever conformed to a physical type, it might well have been the decadent oriental despot whom we see reclining on his funeral pyre in Delacroix's 'The Death of Sardanapalus'.

The painting was first exhibited at the Salon of 1827, and was a remarkable failure. Reviewers in the *Globe* and the *Gazette de France* were as savage as they were urbane. The *Observateur* noted that Delacroix would have had to hire 'two vans to move the furniture of Sardanapalus, three hearses for the dead, and two buses for the living'. In short, it was styleless, technically ignorant, vulgar, ridiculous and confused. But worst of all, it was sexually morbid.

The official reaction was even worse. When the Minister of Fine Arts, Sosthène de La Rochefoucauld, called the painter to his office, the latter was expecting a new commission or honour; instead, the Minister informed him that if he wanted to make a living from the state he would have to stop painting pictures like 'Sardanapalus'. On this occasion, the state refused purchase, and the painting was returned in disgrace to Delacroix's studio, where it remained hidden for the rest of his life.

In the entry he himself wrote for the Salon catalogue Delacroix had described the painting as follows:

> The rebels besiege him in his palace. Reclining on a superb bed at the summit of an immense pyre, Sardanapalus gives the order to his eunuchs and the palace officers to slaughter his women, his pages – even his horses and his favourite dogs, so that nothing that had served his pleasure might survive him . . . Aischeh, a Bactrian woman, not wishing to be put to death by a slave, hanged herself from one of the columns supporting the vaulted ceiling . . . Sardanapalus' cupbearer, Baleah, finally committed the pyre to flames and threw himself upon it.

The source of the Sardanapalus story for Delacroix is often assumed to have been Byron's poem, in which the Assyrian king of Nineveh committed suicide as his city was being stormed by a popular rebellion against his sybaritic régime led by the governor of Media, Arabaces, in the year 612 BC. The ancient source for this story was a lost book called the *Persica* written in the fourth century BC by a Greek writer named Ktesias, who dated the suicide to the year 876. This story was almost certainly invented.

Although Byron was a standard source of sexual fury for the Romantics, the English poet never described a massacre in Sardanapalus' palace. In his account, the king sends his court out of the building to spare them from the self-immolation, and dies alone with a single favourite concubine. The story of the cremation comes from the Greek sources, and in these Sardanapalus is not the masculine figure he is in Byron but a kind of perverse androgyne. In Ktesias, he is a mythic debauchee with some of the attributes of the Assyrian god Sandon, who was a *female* divinity.

Delacroix has not made Sardanapalus androgynous, but he shocked the Salon and exposed himself to later resentment for two other reasons. In the first place, it is now commonplace to view his depictions of massacres of women as fairly simple exposés of his crushing erotic anxieties, anxieties fully apparent in the early pages of his *Journal*. The foreground of 'Sardanapalus' is dominated by the vertical white line of the naked concubine – Oriental Woman at her most blatantly fantastic – having a knife slotted into her clavicle by a henchman who has taken hold of her left arm and is wrenching it backwards. In these two figures we see the use of a common convention among European painters: a contrast between the white skin of the odalisque and the brown or black skin of the servant, the dazzlingly white skin of the Muslim woman here lent carnal brilliance by the proximity of servile ebony. The two most influential examples are perhaps the great 'Odalisque and Slave' of Ingres, where the reclining Venus is straight out of Titian and where the two accompanying figures darken behind her, leaving her half-revealed body pearl-white in the picture's foreground, and the 'Moorish Bath' of Gérôme, where the Arab woman's skin is made to glow under a spatter of points of sunlight while the naked black girl next to her actually touches her with one of her hands.

The picture also indulged in spatial distortions, which were interpreted at the time as technical incompetence, as the testimony of the perspectivist Thénot, who examined the painting, shows:

Mr Delacroix asked me to trace a few monumental lines in his 'Death of Sardanapalus'. All the figures were painted, there was nothing left to do but the architecture. All these figures had been drawn from the same place and at the same height, without him having bothered with the horizon either in the painting or in Nature herself; thus one saw the top of a head when one should have seen the underside of the chin, and subsequently likewise for all the other parts of the body. However, he thought them accurate as drawings since he had drawn them from nature. He should have known that when the model is raised five feet he is not seen in the same way as when he is raised fifteen or twenty feet, for although his position may be the same, the aspect which he presents to the viewer is completely different.

Was this ineptitude truly involuntary? It is well known that when Delacroix set sail for Morocco on 11 January 1832 in the company of the dandy Count Charles de Mornay he was about to experience a revolution in his conception of colour. The Moroccan trip itself is now held to be the catalyst which launched him into a form of painting in which Thénot's Unities were more aggressively exploded than ever before, for his confrontation with the Orient, in whatever form, turned him into one for whom colour was the point of painting. In *A Small Philosophic Dictionary of the Fine Arts* he later wrote: 'Contrary to popular opinion, I would say that colour has a more mysterious and perhaps more powerful influence; it acts, we might say, without our knowledge.'

It is clear that for Delacroix himself, this discovery of the irrational mysticism of colour was associated with Morocco. The orientalist painting he made his own was dominated therefore by three anomalies, which are all present in 'Sardanapalus' and which make it a map of the imagination of sexual pessimism as it drew sustenance from the myth of the Orient. We have the explosive and erotic power of pure colour; we have the Doomed or Enslaved Woman; and lastly we have the horse as symbol of violence, passion and uncontrolled desire.

There are two kinds of impromptu sketch in Delacroix's *Journal* dealing with the 1832 trip to Morocco: naked female torsos, and horses. In one of them the head of a horse even merges nightmarishly with the head and shoulders of a European woman dressed for a garden party. The two subjects were not particularly different, for from Fuseli onwards the horse had been taken as agent of the supernatural, or as a grotesque but picturesque manifestation of instinct. And in that, perhaps horses and women had something in common.

It is curious to note the history of Delacroix's growing interest in the impulsive *equus*. An earlier trip to England had fired his imagination: he had always wanted to go to the land of his beloved Bonington and Constable, and his aristocratic connections made the visit relatively pleasant. True, he found English architecture lumpy and mediocre, and the coarse brutishness of the English proletariat shocked him; as he noted, there was something 'sad and uncouth in all this, which does not fit in with what we have in France'. But when it came to the British horse his enthusiasm overflowed. He learnt to ride on the Edgware Road at Mr Elmore's stable, and there he found that Plato's analogy of the soul to a charioteer careering around with four fiery nags at the bit was all too profound. The English had known this all along: from Stubbs and Fuseli to that same Byron who had been inspired by the slightly absurd story of Mazeppa the Cossack, who was bound to the back of a horse by his lover's Polish count of a husband and carried into the Steppes like a human faggot before being recovered by his beloved.

In the Orient, of course, horses were even better than in England. In fact, they were the *soul* of the Orient. The nineteenth century liked its polar antinomies when it came to East and West (antinomies which are still all too current). These polar clichés were usually subtly anti-Western, for the orientalist needed above all to enter his own fantasy, which was predictably in revolt against the repulsive philistines at home. Hence, where the West was materialist, industrial, self-despoiling, conquest-orientated, rational, analytic and warlike, the East was pacific, spiritual, synthetic, co-operative and pastoral. And as a result of being all these latter, it was also *erotic*.

All of these polarities were poured into the horse. Where the European horse was a disciplined economic instrument or a performing clown, the oriental horse was the animal in nature, violent, unpredictable and slightly mad. There was no question which made the better paintings.

The change in European perceptions of the Islamic horse in particular tell us everything about the changing Western use of the Near East as a vessel of self-flagellating fantasy. When a sixteenth-century French ambassador to the Sublime Porte named Busbequius wrote a long description of horses in the Ottoman Empire, he paid attention above all to their disciplined self-restraint:

There is no Creature so gentle as a Turkish Horse, nor more respectful to his Master or the Groom that dresses him. The reason is because they treat their Horses with great Lenity. They will with their Teeth take up a Staff or Club upon the Road, which their Rider hath let fall, and hold it up to him again; and when they are perfect in this Lesson, then, for their Credit, they have Rings of Silver hung from their Nostrils as a Badge of Honour and good Discipline.

Three hundred years later, however, Lamartine, in his *Voyage en orient*, described a somewhat different Islamic horse:

One has to have visited one of the stables of Damascus, or those of the Emir Beschir, to have a real idea of the Arab horse. This superb and graceful animal loses its beauty, its sweetness and picturesque form when it is transplanted from its native country and its familiar habitudes to our cold climates and the darkness and solitude of our stables. One has to see it at the entrances of the tents of the desert Bedouins, its head

174

between its legs, shaking its long black mane, like a mobile parasol, and sweeping its flanks polished like bronze or silver with the rotating whip of its tail, whose extremity is always dyed purple with henna; one has to see it dressed in sparkling girdles decorated with gold and embroideries of pearls; the head covered with a net of blue or red silk, threaded with gold or silver and with *aiguillettes* which fall from his forehead onto his nostrils and which veils or unveils, with each undulation of his neck, the immense, enflamed, intelligent, sweet and proud globe of his flared eye.

In Lamartine we find described the very horse which occupies much of the foreground of the 'Death of Sardanapalus'. For whereas the sixteenth-century observer was preoccupied with the *behaviour* of the horse, its inner domesticity, what interested the nineteenth-century man was the horse as *picture*, as visual splendour embodying by means of its intense colour and the fluidity of its form the sexual energy of the Orient. Lamartine cannot resist evoking the coldness, solitude and darkness of the European stable, a place where it is difficult to imagine the impetuous Arab stallion mating. Lamartine goes on to amplify his portrait of the Eastern horse by describing the animals *en masse*; they become a huge, broiling organism somewhat like a crowd of people, which even reacts with suspicion on seeing Lamartine's

European clothes, before slowly familiarizing itself with him. Lamartine concludes mystically:

> The mobility and transparence of the physiognomy of these horses is an incredible thing, incredible that is if one has not witnessed it oneself. All their thoughts manifest themselves in their eyes and in the convulsive movement of their cheeks, their lips, their nostrils, with as much evidence, with as much character and mobility, as the impressions of the soul upon the face of a child.

The child has often been the model of the non-European ideal: were the Noble Savages not admirable children? The essential characteristic of the child is spontaneity, and by celebrating the oriental horse the Western orientalist celebrated the infantile spontaneity, which he assumed was the root of the oriental's spiritual health.

The *health* of the horse, and of the exotic humans who reflect its sexual dynamism, becomes in turn one side of yet another polar cliché: that of the *diseased* nature of the West. For against the horse with all its flowing primeval qualities could be pitted the awful machine and the moral zombies who stood in its shadow.

All of the scholars, painters, translators and anthropological missionaries who hurled themselves into the East from the latter half of the eighteenth century onwards were charged with a mission to find a civilization, or traces of such, which was a reverse image of their own. The East India Company took hundreds of English idealists reeling from the supposed horrors of industrialism to the vicinity of Bombay, where Warren Hastings set out to revive classical Hindu culture with the establishment of Vedic colleges. In his wake orientalists like Colebrook and Jones produced translations of the *Bhagavadgita*, invented a myth of a Hindu golden age, the *Ramraj*, and instilled in the rising Indian intelligentsia a conviction of pre-industrial spiritual wisdom.

For the Enlightenment, however, the two sources of orientalist fantasy were the Muslim Near East and Ming China. What were the characteristics of these two civilizations, which Voltaire and company had, of course, never visited? Luxury and serenity. Even today, a modern historical atlas dubiously assures the reader that, up to the time of Voltaire, Ottoman Turkey represented a domain of luxurious living which Europeans could only marvel at and envy.

Luxury and serenity give rise to a certain sex life, too. Delacroix obviously found Muslim women perfect because they inhabited the world of the harem. And it was in the harem that the nineteenth-century Europeans found their curious ideal of femininity. But what is obvious is that, however accurately a painter like Gérôme could depict the baths he had actually visited in Cairo in

1868 (transmitting to the reader of his accounts all the sense of awe and wonder which access to the forbidden world of women inflicted upon him as he passed through 'a mysterious door'), what was actually being created was a vision of what Lenoir, who accompanied him to the baths, called 'an opera in five, very distinct and regulated acts' – an opera, and nothing else.

Most of the painters who roamed around the Near East from the 1830s onwards – Lewis, Roberts, Guillamet, Francis Frith – were photographers with brushes. They were the oil-wielding counterparts of the photographer Maxime du Camp. But even in the Dickensian scenes of Turkish street life painted by Wilkie or the meticulously rendered dramas of Cairene salons and schoolrooms left to us by Lewis, or the luminous realism of the snapshots of Jaffa markets and carpet bazaars executed by Bauenfeind or Müller, the *fantastic* impulses of the occidental are impossible to erase. Even when the idealism of Voltaire refused to negotiate any reality other than the writer's own nation, it did so with a charm which disarmed and disarms all and sundry. For the European tendency to fantasize about the Orient also took the form of a slavish and pseudo–documentary admiration which made everything east of the Sublime Porte superior.

Europeans began by admiring the military organization of the Ottomans. From this they went on to idealize everything else in Ottoman society, which became a kind of portable mental model of sobriety, rationality and efficiency. The Ottoman Empire, in other words, became a mystic blueprint for everything Europeans wanted to be, just as Japan is today, regardless of what the admired society is actually like. And from admiring janissary artillery to believing in the sexual prowess and completeness of the Muslim woman was not as large a step as might be imagined. The gushing eulogies of Ottoman infantry that we find in Busbequius are not so far removed from the paeans to the Egyptian courtesan Katim Husuk in the letters of Flaubert.

It comes as a surprise to realize how self-deluding these exercises have always been. The Ottoman ambassador to Paris in 1720, Mehmet Effendi, has left the only detailed and inquisitive account by a Turkish intellectual of early eighteenth-century France, and his descriptions of that country contradict at every point the awe-struck effusions of the *philosophes*. What did Mehmet Effendi notice about the French? Their technical sophistication, their complex and rigorous administration and their wealth; in other words, exactly the things that were supposed to be the privilege of Ottomans. The spectacular architecture of the palaces, which were vast by Ottoman standards, particularly impressed him, and he set out to reproduce them in Istanbul on his return. Effendi also introduced into the Ottoman Empire the first printing presses from France, issuing warnings concerning the backwardness of Ottoman science which would have astounded the French intellectuals cooing over the opulence of Eastern knowledge.

Mehmet Effendi was an urbane and shrewd traveller who was the exact opposite of the European orientalist. As a real oriental rather than a synthetic one he showed little interest in comparisons of putative 'spirituality': he was more interested in clocks, glass-making techniques and cannon technology. Nor did he find the French aesthetically inferior. Most Ottoman gardens, architecture and design of the Tulip Era were conscious imitations of the French, rather than the other way round. One area, however, in which Mehmet Effendi emphatically drew the line was the treatment of women. He was astonished at the insolent behaviour of French women, which is to say, their relative mobility. Almost in disbelief he wrote:

In France, esteem for women prevails among men. The women can do what they want and go where they desire. To the lowest, the best gentlemen would show more regard and respect than necessary. In these lands, women's commands are enforced. So much so that France is the paradise of women. They have no hardships or troubles at all – it is said that they obtain their wishes and desires without any resistance whatsoever.

The oriental was dismayed by the relative freedom of the European woman, or at least her ability in a society such as that of eighteenth-century France to dominate salon intellectual life, while the European male admired the submission and sequestered secrecy of the oriental woman. And in essence, the dismay of one and of the other was identical.

The orientalist's need for a world that was both different and preferable burns in modern literature with undiminished intensity. Perhaps the most debonair and ludicrous priest of self-hating orientalism was Pierre Loti, in whom one can clearly see all the main features of that semi-religion: the East as a spectacle; the superiority of the nomad and the pre-industrial; the hateful face of Modern Civilization; and the pessimism which decides that the latter is ugly, soulless and sexless. As he wrote in *Turkey in Agony*: 'There are other things in life besides factories, railways, opening up trade, shrapnel and neurasthenia.'

Like the Jew, the modern West is a compendium of evils and spiritual discomforts. And if the West is inert in the realm of the senses, then the ideal of vitality must lie in its negative image, the Orient. Needless to say, Loti makes no evocation whatsoever of any other aspect of early twentieth-century European culture. He does not say, 'There is more to life than literature, theoretical physics, Cubist painting, symphonic music, art nouveau furniture and Symbolist poetry.' No, it is *railways, factories, neurasthenia*. Bankruptcy, sham, pseudo-progress.

In the chapter entitled 'After the Fire' Loti

describes old Stanboul in a passage that sums up the orientalist attitude to the world:

> Yesterday there survived a town which, as if by a miracle, had almost preserved its identity since the days of Eastern glory. The noise of engine-whistles and the clanking of vehicles, which are such features of our modern capitals, were still kept at bay. Life was flowing there, thoughtful and discreet, tempered by faith; men still prayed there, and thousands of uniform little tombs of exquisite shape peopled the shady places, gently reminiscent of a death without terror. That was Stanboul. Nor was it at the end of the world. It was in Europe, scarcely three days from our feverish and nerve-racking Paris.

Hatred of railways seemed to be a code of honour among orientalists. The greatest literary orientalist, Flaubert, was a famous hater of them. On the one hand there were glory, splendour, *nostalgie de la boue*, expert courtesans and marvellous sunsets; on the other . . . *railways*. Loti did not want the Bulgarians to retake Istanbul because they would impose upon it 'the ugliness of modernism'.

Mystery and railways were obviously incompatible, and if these two things are mutually exclusive, then so are neurasthenia and sexual health. In another book on Egypt, Loti continually trades in the cliché of the tranquil, content Easterners, 'so graceful in their rags, so mysterious in their age-old immobility':

> And it is not difficult to understand, perhaps, how the spectacle of our troubles, our despairs, our miseries, in these new ways in which our lot is cast, should make them reflect and turn again to the tranquil dream of their ancestors.

The images of industrial culture that Loti uses are already familiar to us, since they are essentially those foisted upon the arch-capitalist, the Jew. It is a vision informed by sexual pessimism, for the modern age is seen as a waster of instinct and the touchstone of authenticity is the past, just as it was to be for Reich and Lawrence. Loti barely tries to disguise this fact. Like Flaubert, he was ravished by the delectable sensation of moving backwards in time. The orientalist's romanticism is absolutely standard in that it is continually haunted by the possibility of travel as time-travel. 'All this savours of the past,' Loti swoons on almost every page. And where does time-travel lead if taken to its logical extreme, if not to the Garden of Eden itself? Painters in the Orient thought that they were moving in three-dimensional reconstructions of biblical Antiquity – a feeling very clear in a man like Holman Hunt. But what lay beyond that Antiquity was something even older, a purity even more uncontaminated: the Garden situated somewhere in the vicinity of the Persian Gulf.

The Orientalists were the precursors of romantic Third Worldists. What made them different was the particular version of Eastern sexuality which they wanted to believe in. Of course, the tumult and bloodshed of Sardanapalus' palace have little to do with the grace of the Garden. The similarity of the two lies in the feeling of nostalgia which both evoke. Delacroix felt nostalgia for oriental women because, as Mehmet Effendi had noted, French women didn't fit the bill. They weren't sexualized in the same way as these women of the past, who, probably because of their lack of exposure to railways, were purely sexual, their being condensed into one lyrical purpose. As Loti noted of the women of Egypt, they were a vision of the past, like 'the daughters of Hellas'. And what gave them 'nobility of attitude and carriage'? Their submission to instinct.

Flaubert's descriptions of the dancers Kuchuk Hanem and the Nubian Azizeh in Egypt in 1850 betray, in the first place, the writer's love of the conjunction of the brutal and the fantastic (of Kuchuk Hanem's companion dancer Bambeh he notes subtly in passing that her eyes 'were only slightly diseased'), and in the second, his conviction of the sexual superiority of the oriental woman over the Western. His nights with Kuchuk at Esna he represents as his sexual apogee. We first see her on the stairs in the courtyard of her house, 'surrounded by light and standing against the background of the blue sky, a woman in pink trousers. Above, she wore only a dark violet gauze.' He then describes her as follows:

> Kuchuk is a tall, splendid creature, lighter in colouring than an Arab; she comes from Damascus; her skin, particularly on her body, is slightly coffee-coloured. When she bends, her flesh ripples into bronze ridges. Her eyes are dark and enormous, her eyebrows black, her nostrils open and wide; heavy shoulders, full, apple-shaped breasts. She wore a large tarboosh, ornamented on the top with a convex gold disc, in the middle of which was a small green stone imitating emerald . . . She has one upper incisor, right, which is beginning to go bad.

What excites Flaubert about Kuchuk is that oriental proximity of emeralds and rotted incisors. In his travel notes, he constantly admires the bits of gold attached to bodies festering with sores. 'Kuchuk's dance is brutal,' he notes, with nothing of the grace of the transvestites he had seen in Cairo. Or was it because all beautiful women dance badly? 'She squeezes her bare breasts together with her jacket.' He then adds, 'I have seen this dance on old Greek vases.'

Commentators on the 'Father of the Moustache', as Flaubert was known to the Egyptians, never fail to see in Kuchuk previsions of Salammbô, and are fascinated by the domestic scene in which Flaubert describes falling asleep with her hand in his, the courtesan snoring, 'a triangular gleam, the colour of pale metal, on her beautiful forehead', her little dog sleeping on his silk jacket:

> I gave myself over to intense reverie, full of reminiscence. Feeling of her stomach against my buttocks . . . Another time I dozed off with my fingers passed through her necklace, as though to hold her should she awake. I thought of Judith and Holofernes sleeping together . . . We told each other a great many things by pressure.

But what is most striking in these passages is Flaubert's love of prostitution, and of the Orient as a culture of prostitution, at least one in which the ethos of the prostitute was glorified. 'It may be a perverted taste,' he wrote elsewhere:

> but I love prostitution, and for itself too, quite apart from its carnal aspects. My heart begins to pound every time I see one of those women in low-cut dresses walking under the lamplight in the rain, just as monks in their corded robes have always excited some deep, ascetic corner of my soul. The idea of prostitution is a meeting place of so many elements – lust, bitterness, complete absence of human contact, muscular frenzy, the clink of gold – that to peer into it deeply makes one reel. One learns so many things in a brothel, and feels such sadness, and dreams so longingly of love! . . .

Isn't this an inadvertently accurate description of all women in orientalist art? 'The Death of Sardanapalus' contains six dying concubines. It should properly be called 'The Massacre of the Courtesans'. Why does the oriental courtesan-concubine evoke the feelings described by Flaubert above? Because she is disposable. Why is she sculpturally tragic? Because cruelty descends upon her at any moment.

The woman without a carapace of civil liberties is able to merge into that intense, irrational world which disobeys the polite laws of perspective, and because she is the object of man's will (the slave who – as in the Ottoman seraglio – is either *godze*, 'in the Lord's eye', or *ikbal*, 'taken to bed') she is the very antithesis of European reason, brothel sanitation legislation, and of course railways. The Orient was the colourful refutation of democracy and the Rights of Man, which as we know lead irresistibly to utter philistinism. And it was the suffering of the oriental woman which gave her world its charming integrity.

The snapshot of these strange contradictions which Delacroix painted indeed had its counterpart in reality. The Pakistani author Mazharul Haq Khan, in a book called *Purdah and Polygamy*, describes how the sultans disposed of excess numbers of inconvenient concubines and wives when the harems became too crowded:

Countless women were killed by irate husbands

all over the Muslim world in the Middle Ages, but the Ottoman Turks proved to be the cruellest in this respect. Their usual technique of disposing of an unfaithful or unwanted wife or woman was to sew her up in a sack and throw her into a well, stream, river or sea nearby, to be drowned to death. Writing of the Imperial harems of the Ottoman Sultans, N.M. Penzer says, 'The drowning of one or two women would attract no notice at all, and everything would be carried out with silence and dispatch. The Kislar Agha takes them to the Bostanji-bashi, under whose direction the hapless females are placed in sacks weighted with stones. The bostanji, to whom the duty of drowning them is committed, board a small rowing-boat to which is attached by a rope a smaller one in which the women are placed. They then row towards the open water opposite Seraglio point, and by several dexterous jerks of the rope cause the boat to capsize. A eunuch accompanies the bostanji and reports to the Kislar Agha the fulfilment of his orders.'

At times, however, a mass drowning would take place on the discovery of some plot to depose the Sultan or similar grave offence. As many as 300 women have been drowned on such an occasion. The most terrible case was during the reign of Ibrahim (1640–48), who after one of his debauches suddenly decided to drown his complete harem for the fun of getting a new one later. Accordingly several hundred women were seized and thrown into the Bosphorus. Only one escaped. She was picked up by a passing vessel and ultimately reached Paris.

The orientalist fascination with women dying, in captivity or as dancing spectacle, is not simply a matter of sexual sadism or the enjoyment of power as a stimulant. It is more perverse even than that. The orientalist craved, and craves, immersion in a world where aesthetic beauty is multiform, unlimited and, as it were, infinitely plastic. It takes the form one moment of an exquisite tile or a courtyard; the next it melts into a horse; and then, a moment later, it takes the form of a woman dying with a knife entering her neck. Delacroix deliberately suspended the laws of perspective because his subject matter made it inevitable. This world, the Orient, is one of mercurial colour, with no questions asked. And no questions are asked because it is a fantasy which has to express contempt for reality. It is a moralizing *design*.

At its most savage, as in writers like Loti and, today, Juan Goytisolo, orientalism takes the aesthetic of the East as something untouchable. Goytisolo, that most archetypal Spaniard, flagellates his homeland with a rhetorical cultural treachery which borders on childish anti-paternal escapism. He puts on his turban to hate. Like Loti, he does not ask questions about Islam, for the latter is essentially Sufic, pure music, pure colour. It is unreal, whatever the expertise of the writer in local colour. What matters is to rape the Fatherland.

When sexuality is inserted into this *artistic enterprise*, all of its most nightmarish possibilities are brought within the dim realm of the possible. It becomes as infantile and unreal as the fantasy it is surrounded by. And how could Woman be the apex of this dynamic and dangerous zoo, this boiling menagerie which was as much taken with lion hunts, massacres and carnivorous duels, without being herself as unreal as Sardanapalus?

10
The Androgyne

Throughout its history, sexual pessimism has been nothing if not inventive. It alights upon one victim and then another, ascribing to all of them basically quite similar attributes. We have seen that this pessimism in the West is Gnostic, but we have also seen that it is not uniquely Western. What is uniquely Western is only the marriage of sexual pessimism and the myth of Eden – that, and a way of seeing the body which penetrates through its outer shell of grace.

But was it not the case that European sexual pessimism not only led the physical body to be regarded as that 'walking grave' which the Christian–Gnostic tradition reviled, but also led to its invisible instincts being regarded in the same way? All Christians lived in walking graves but some, as we have seen again and again, were more gravelike than others. And what has ever seemed more peculiar to Christian pessimism than its hatred of homosexuality?

The last figure in our series, then, is the catamite – or, rather, to approach the fear at its root, the androgyne. Certainly, if we all have horrific bodies clinging to our souls which we should all be thankful to get rid of one day, one could hardly imagine the horror of the mutant body, the hermaphrodite. Wouldn't he/she be condemned to tortures a thousand times worse than even the sufferings of St Bartholomew on the wall of the Sistine Chapel? And could one ever imagine the pain inflicted upon the perverted soul by this ghastly trick of nature, a misadventure which could only be explained by the wit of demons?

Western theology has a long history of hostility to homosexuality. Aquinas described it not as an illness or a mere defect, but as an actual corruption of the soul. Yet Catholics had borrowed some of their hostility, surprisingly enough, from Arab doctors such as Avicenna, who described homosexual love in the *Canon* as a 'mental perversity'. The great doctor even prescribed a course of torture to shock the sick man out of his evil ways, a course which would destroy the perverted desire by means of the application of physical and moral brutality: hunger, depression, isolation and flagellation. These remedies, needless to say, were enthusiastically taken up by some Western readers of Avicenna. The fifteenth-century doctor Jacques Despars prescribed more or less the same thing.

In both Islam and Christianity, it is noticeable

that lesbians are treated much less harshly than male homosexuals. The usual adjectives applied to men – *shameful, detestable* and *vile* – were hardly ever used against women. Lesbians merely went to purgatory, where we sometimes meet them in medieval art and literature, calmly working off their sentences.

Compare this leniency to the thundering of Albertus on the 'contagious' nature of male homosexuality: 'It must be said that the deformity of sins is often measured in accordance with three criteria, namely grace, reason and nature. The sin which is against grace, reason and nature is the greatest: that is the case with sodomy.'

Why, then, was this sexual sin seen as more heinous than any other?

The roots to this nausea are ancient and complex. Contrary to many conceptions of the ancient world, Classical Antiquity did not condone homosexuality without reservation. We have already seen that the Romans detested passivity in sexual matters, and despised passive homosexuals, who were known as *impudicus* or *diatithemonos*. As Paul Veyne has shown, the Romans too condemned homosexuality when it was effeminate. The active partner, being virile, was above approach. But the other, the passive, was little more than a slave. In other words, when the homosexual was manlike he was acceptable. But what was definitely *un*acceptable was what the Japanese novelist Mishima called the 'feminization of the male'.

The man who was a surrogate woman was more disgusting than anything in creation. Veyne even gives the example of the Emperor Claudius, who disdained having a passive homosexual executed because it would have soiled the executioner's sword.

Hatred of effeminacy is a deep neurosis in countless societies. Mishima talked endlessly of the 'feminization of the male' as one would of a nightmare. It is one of the curiosities of his attitude to his own culture that he should so have adored Greek and Roman culture, and disliked so intensely the woodprint art of the Floating World, in which not only are *kabuki* stars glorified in all their androgynous glory, but even normal men and women are depicted as androgynous Siamese twins. His disgust was very intense, and it is explored at some length in his commentary on the *Hagakure*, the *samurai* codebook written by Jocho Yammomoto at the end of the seventeenth century:

> One can see evidence of this trend in *ukiyo-ye* [Floating World] prints of the eighteenth-century master Haranobu Suzuki. The couples snuggling together as they sit on the edge of the veranda gazing at plum blossoms so resemble each other in hair styles, the cut and pattern of their clothes, the very expression of their faces that no matter how you examine them, no matter from what angle, it is impossible to tell which is the man and which is the woman. During the age in which

194

Hagakure was written, this trend had already begun.

He then goes on to quote from Jocho himself at length. The passage is called 'The Female Pulse':

I heard this from an acquaintance of mine. Apparently, a Dr Kyoan once made the following statement: 'In medicine we distinguish between men and women by attributing to them the principles of yin and yang, and medical treatment originally differed accordingly. The pulse is also different. Over the last fifty years, however, the pulse of men has gradually become the same as that of women. Since noticing this phenomenon, I have considered it proper to treat eye diseases of male patients with the method normally appropriate to the pulse of women patients. When I try applying to male patients the cures appropriate to men, they produce no effect whatsoever. The world is indeed entering a degenerate stage; men are losing their virility and becoming just like women. This is an unshakeable truth which I have learned from first-hand experience. I have decided to keep it a secret from the world at large.' When with this story in mind I look around me at the men of today, I often think to myself, *Aha, there goes an example of the female pulse.*

Mishima calls this a 'scathing passage' and quotes

it without the slightest trace of irony. Forlornly, he utters his contempt for 'youths in coffee houses' dressed in effeminate clothes. Once, when he was dancing in a homosexual club in his youth, a casual partner made a derogatory remark about his physique. Mortified, the proud writer – anguished by the thought of the feminization of his own body – set out to master the techniques of the gym and turn his body into 'the orchard of the soul'. In other words, to turn it into a fantasy of male beauty which, when it was mutilated and disembowelled by the act of *seppuku* with which Mishima ended his own life, would be as beautiful in death as it had been in life.

The androgyne was celebrated in Japanese culture prior to industrialization. It was endemic in the *kabuki*, and during the Genroku period (1688–1703) the androgynous boy became the arbiter of beauty. But the *shudo*, or idealized homosexual love, which the *samurai* practised was not androgynous in nature. True, the *samurai* was advised always to carry rouge and powder with him, and to make himself up before going into battle. But the *bushido* way of the warrior was narcissistic in a different way, with the cosmetic beauty of the male cultivated for one purpose: the creation of a beautiful corpse.

Why, in any case, did the homosexual aesthetic collapse in the following centuries? The root of this decline is almost always imputed to the rising influence of industrial Christianity, especially after the Meiji Restoration and the Industrial Revolution which followed it, lasting until about 1910. But in fact homosexuality was in decline long before Commodore Parry arrived in Tokyo Bay with his black ships. The Tempo reforms of 1843 stamped out male prostitution with no reference at all to Christian interdictions, and Japan's industrialization was in any case never Christianized. The Japanese scholar Tsuneo Watanabe sees this modernization, however, as instrumental to the switching of beauty from men to women, for the same thing has happened in the West. It is a transformation whereby men become greyer and more anonymous, while women become more physically charismatic. This reversal is taken to such extremes in industrial societies that women can be said to 'monopolize beauty'. It is this which frustrates the male homosexual aesthete, as it did Mishima. Watanabe cites an interesting passage from the German ethnologist Eibl-Eibesfeldt in which the latter describes the de-eroticizing of the male, or what he calls *Vermausgrauung* – a making grey, like a mouse. After noting that in small societies the male imposes himself through peacockery, he goes on rather sadly:

It's not at all the same in an anonymous crowd. All these imposing behaviours provoke aggression in others which is not moderated by personal acquaintance. They gravely disturb communal life and to avoid this, man conforms to mass society by depriving himself of virile and imposing displays. We see in all civilizations a process of *Vermausgrauung* of the men. Their dress becomes simple, masculine jewellery is reduced and arms are completely abandoned . . . The less one is noticed, the better it is.

The anti-androgyne complex achieves supremacy also because, with the conceiving of the first dictionaries of sexual perversion, the homosexual and the androgyne can be ascribed to specific pathologies. They are peeled away from normal life. And it is also true that this medical demonization is far more ruthless to men than to women. A man dressed in woman's clothing is a far greater object of ridicule than a woman in man's. In the early psychiatric texts, the *perversions* are male, with the female ones added on afterwards for symmetry.

Although homosexuality in Japan enjoyed a few revivals, its decline during the twentieth century was steady. And for Mishima, acutely aware that the whole traditional culture of *bushido* was bound up with *shudo*, this decline could only be seen as synonymous with Japan's accelerating cultural subordination to the West.

But how does Mishima's protest at this 'degeneration' account for his own pessimism, a sexual pessimism which in his hands seems wholly and ancestrally Japanese? The nostalgia for the way of the *samurai* was nothing if not a nostalgia for the melding of physical beauty and death. Dr Kyoan was pessimistic about men's pulses. They had changed. They had *deteriorated*. A sexual transformation was putting an ever widening distance between people and the golden age. And the pessimism regarding homosexuals in Japan was perhaps felt as a kind of restoration, a return to a pre-Genroku period of manliness and energy. Whatever the reason, the power of nostalgia to create sexual pessimism is as clear in this culture as it is in that of the West. For when a society looks, as it were, over its shoulder at its own past, it cannot help dreaming that it sees its own perfection. The androgyne was glorified by the theatrical culture of Tokugawa Japan, but for the nostalgic in the mould of Mishima this glorification was nothing more than an interlude. The boy–girl was a corruption, as it was in the West. And the phobia of the latter for all things effeminate seems at once somewhat less unique than it is so often claimed to be. It is true, however, that in the West there was little glorification in the first place. In its stead, there was scientific awe. The androgyne was both magical and terrifying. Was he/she, though, another basilisk-like creature in the mould of the witch, the freakish plaything of Satan? Or was he/she a curious reminder of the suspicions of anatomists, whose eccentricity had little to do with the excoriation of the homosexual?

It should be noticed that in neither culture did anyone think to measure this exotic animal's pulse.

*   *   *

In one of his papers the Mexican doctor Gonzalez-Crussi notes that Antoninus of Florence had once concluded that men and women were divided by so many differences that it was impossible that they could belong to the same species. This witty doctor, however, has also recounted the statement of Aristophanes in Plato's *Symposium* to the effect that the primeval race, progenitor of us all, was androgynous, a bizarre creature with two faces looking in opposite directions, and two sets of each limb: a unique distribution of bodily parts enabling him to move with the locomotive agility of a human crab. Best of all, we are told, the genitals too were in pairs. The combinations would have been enviable, and these lucky androgynes would have perfectly understood the cryptic observation of another doctor, this time a Viennese: 'When two people make love, four people are involved.'

What happened to the sexually gifted, inventive and probably tortured androgynes? Is it really true that they displeased the gods and were therefore severed – as Plato says, 'like sorb apples' – from top to bottom with the dreaded surgical knife of Zeus?

Is it really true that there were contingency plans to slice the severed androgyne once again, into four parts, in the eventuality of further transgressions? Or did the fabulous unicorn of the world of sex disappear, like the Anthropophagi, into the deserts of Ethiopia, with an enigmatic grin on its face, indifferent to the fate of its bastard cousins, the males and the females?

The sheer realism of Aristophanes' account of the androgyne is too compelling. He says it went 'whirling around like a clown turning cartwheels when it ran', that with eight legs it could go at incredible speed, that it was descended from the Moon (which partakes of either sex), and that when split its two halves yearned so ferociously for one another that Zeus was obliged to rearrange the genitals frontally so that they could at least satisfy themselves once in a while. He then goes on to explain that in this way man could satisfy man, or produce children if he happened to encounter a woman. For if a man derives from the male half of the original androgyne he will be attracted to men, and so with women. Only those who are 'a slice of the hermaphrodite sex' will be attracted to the opposite.

The woman who is a slice of the original female is attracted by other women rather than by men – in fact she is a lesbian – while men who are slices of the male are followers of the male, and show their masculinity throughout their boyhood by the way they make friends with men, and the delight they take in lying beside them and being taken in their arms. And these are the most hopeful of the nation's youth, for theirs is the most virile constitution.

Plato's diagnosis is enough to seduce any physiologist: the heterosexual is a slice of the hermaphrodite rather than being a pure male or female. His or her desire is mongrel, being a paste-up of two sexes. And Gonzalez-Crussi follows the opinion of Aristophanes that desire, far from being a quest for dominion, is a yearning for the infrangible wholeness of the androgyne, 'the very embodiment of immortality'.

Yet throughout history, far from inspiring respect and affection, the androgyne seems to have provoked little less than a whole breed of sexual pessimism of its own. Gonzalez-Crussi himself provides us with a depressing list of ambiguous characters who have surfaced for brief and miserable moments in different ages and left nothing behind them but lugubrious memories of heresy: Marguerite Malaure, the tragic hermaphrodite of seventeenth-century France forced by law to dress as a man and persecuted for the unpardonable sin of possessing both male and female sexual organs; Anne Grandjean, who at puberty suddenly ceased being an angelic little girl and promptly turned into a boy, married happily under the name of Jean-Baptiste and then narrowly escaped being publicly hanged for infringing the public code following the depositions of royal physicians dumbfounded by his possession in equal measure of the contradictory organs; James Allen, the famous 'impostor' of nineteenth-century England who married a woman, lived with her happily and then was found upon her death not to have been all that she seemed. More than the stories of transvestite adventurers like the infamous Count Balmori of Mexico City, the case histories of these sexual migrants provide us simultaneously with reasons to discharge affectionate sympathy and the vicarious thrill of theatrical spectacle. We are fascinated and repelled by them. They destroy the immaculate and bivalved world of sex around whose magnet we revolve.

The demonologists lost no time in realizing this. In the seventeenth century, Francisco Guazzo, in his *Demonologie*, recorded many examples of what he took to be spontaneous conversion from one sex to another, undoubtedly diabolically inspired. He writes:

Cornelius Gemma inquires into the mutation of the feminine into the masculine sex, and the masculine into the feminine, which is admitted by modern physicians to be natural. We read of many women who have become men. Hippocrates writes that at Abdera Phaetula the wife of Pitheus had borne him children; but when her husband was sent into exile her menstrual courses ceased and she was smitten with terrible pains all over her body, and acquired the physical features of a man. He says that the same thing happened to Anamisia the wife of Gorgippus at Thasos. Livy tells the same story in Book 24 [*De spoletana Muliere*]. Pliny says that it is no fable that women are changed into men. Martin Delrio uses the following words (quoting from Pliny in *Historia naturalis*, VII): 'I myself saw in Africa L. Cossicius, a Tisdritanian citizen, changed into a woman on his wedding day.'

One can only imagine the reaction of the bride. Guazzo goes on to give authentic case histories of this enigmatic and dramatic transformation. One of them is taken from the *Jardin de las flores curiosas* of Torquemada:

In the town of Ezgueira in Portugal, about nine leagues from Coimbra, there lived a nobleman who had a daughter named Maria Pacheco. When this girl was at the age when a woman's monthly courses usually begin, instead of a fluid excretion there broke or otherwise grew from those parts a virile member; and so, from being a girl she suddenly became a public young man endowed with virility, and assumed the name of Manoel Pacheco. He then took ship for India and endured much hardship and performed great deeds as a soldier. Returning to his country he married a noble wife: yet Amatus the Portuguese, writing in his *Centuries*, makes no mention of any children, but says that he remained unbearded and with a feminine cast of appearance, these being indications of imperfect virility. Finally Torquemada adds that he heard this from a most trustworthy friend of great authority.

In another Spanish case, Guazzo describes a mis-treated wife who ran away from home, disguised herself as a man-servant and one day turned into a man – 'either because of the efficacy of her natural heat or through imagination induced and strengthened by her continuous masculine clothing and work . . .' He concludes his account of spon-taneous androgyny as follows:

> At Eboli, a girl had been betrothed for four years. On the first night of her marriage she went to bed with her husband: but either owing to the friction or to some other unknown cause, when the hymen which gave her the appearance of a woman was broken a male organ stood out. She then went home and sued in the Courts for a return of her dowry, and was thereafter reckoned as a man.
>
> If this can come about naturally, as so many authors maintain, I should think that with God's permission it is possible to the ddevil, relying upon natural causes.

Androgyny in demonology seems to confirm the believer's shrewd suspicion that the world is a pliable and untrustworthy place where everything is not as it seems. A place where the Devil is at home.

At the end of his own sombre essay, Gonzalez-Crussi makes the following remark:

> Understanding of sexual differentiation has become the sole avenue for cognition of the forms of human existence, which up to now has been dependent upon our weak perceptions. Descartes, that French gentleman who taught the world the road to certainty, came up with a quaint allegory: We look through the window at the street below, and persuade ourselves that we see Mary and John – the rich subjectivity, the intricate texture of two human beings. But what we see is *chapeaux et manteaux, rien de plus*. Hats and coats, nothing else. So it is with the sexes.

The interior warp that gives feelings their instinctual tension rests upon the most fragile of premises. The human *conceptus* remains undifferentiated until the age of eleven weeks, and even in maturity the sexual organs that cause the race catastrophically and delectably to bifurcate are not as different as they were imagined to be.

The American researcher Josephine Lowndes Sevely has become the first woman to name an individual part of the human anatomy, and this female first in scientific nomenclature relates to the clitoris: the male version. Lowndes contends not only that the male possesses a clitoris, but that it is even morphologically extremely similar to its better known homologue. The drawings of clitoral dissections by Regnier de Graaf and Sabotta which she uses to illustrate her claim do indeed show fork-shaped organs of remarkably analogous structure, with greater bifurcation in the female being the principal difference. Lowndes goes on to show that the male and female generative organs are in fact structurally almost identical, one being a kind of folded-in or folded-out version of the other. The constituent elements of these organs are all present in both sexes: both are equipped with a glans, a sexually active urethra, bulbospongiosum, pubococcygeus and prostatic glands. The same corpora cavernosa. The same foreskin the prepuce in the male, the labia minora in the female. Even the unwieldy scrotum finds its unexpected homologue in the fleshy labia majora.

And the clitoral element which bears the name of the discoverer of unknown regions? The 'Lowndes' Crown', a kind of cap at the tip of the explosive and enigmatic organ.

Opinions on the homologous nature of the sexual organs have been wayward over the centuries. We have seen how medieval map-makers of the genitals represented male and female as interchangeable, a legacy of the hunt for analogy typical of Greek medicine. It is now fashionable to revive this passion for analogy, for obvious reasons, and sometimes, by extension, to cast a favourable eye over the pre-Renaissance culture which produced it. The mischievous Renaissance clove us into two spellbound halves by giving the clitoris to woman and sundering her from everything male . . . the medieval world, on the other hand, immersed in the wholeness of a spiritual order which had not been cracked by dreadful Western rationalism, offered the splendid 'one sex model'.

But the medieval insistence on analogy, symmetry, order and unity – pleasantly harmonious from a safe distance – was also a prison. The female might have sexual organs identical to the male's, as Galen said she did, but the analogical mind also asserted that her womb, like a pig's, was covered with hair, a dogma whose repressive repercussions we have mentioned. The anatomists of the Renaissance could have done nothing but reject a series of magical dogmas which in most cases did not cohere with clinical experience. The medieval world-view was coherent and all-encompassing, metaphysically comforting, because people were not allowed to look inside corpses any more than they were permitted to make the earth rotate around the sun. This 'wholeness', so pined after by naively nostalgic historians of science like Fritjof Capra and so aesthetically pleasing from the outside (and from a comfortable distance of five hundred years), was as claustrophobic and cruel as it was spiritually compensatory. Medicine by analogy and textual hearsay yielded surprising perceptions, but for the wrong reasons – and hence its futility eventually overwhelmed it.

All this should be borne in mind when turning to Lowndes's appeal to the Galenic anatomy.

Claiming the Greek as her progenitor, she provides us with a cross-section of the vagina from Vesalius' *Fabrica* of 1543, pointing out that, though Vesalius challenged Galen, he was nevertheless unable to digress significantly from his views on the reproductive organs. It is indeed curious how male the dissected female organ actually looks. Without knowing which it was beforehand, the casual observer would almost certainly hesitate before assuming which sex it belonged to. Lowndes then quotes Galen himself: 'All the male genital parts are also found in women. There is not any difference except for one point . . . that is, that the female parts are internal and those of the male are external, taking their origin in the region called the perineum.' (*De usu partibus*, Book XIV)

The investigation and naming of the various parts of the intricate structure of the clitoris were carried out during the sixteenth century. Realdo Colombo extended the rapidly expanding realm of science to the hitherto unknown recesses of the labia minora. Fallopio, besides carrying out his pioneering work on the prestigious tubes that now bear his name, began to revolt against Galen's assumptions by pairing the penis with the clitoris, rather than seeing the male apparatus and the vagina as alternative versions of the same organ. The clitoris, paradoxically, was set to acquire a distinctive anatomical life of its own as woman's special organ, the unique appendage which guaranteed her difference from men. The claim of Lowndes is that this mutation in anatomical history (which no one among the Renaissance anatomists was aware of) was the result of a botched translation from Arabic versions of Galen's original: the term *al bathara* in the medical works of Avicenna or Ali ibn Sina, meaning 'clitoris', is rendered in the pages of Fallopio as both 'penis' and 'clitoris', a nuance unintended in the original. It was natural for Fallopio, the first dissector of the clitoris, to regard it as in some way a smaller, stunted version of the male member, but not as an identical organ. And while the homologous nature of the two is still noticed, the similarity of their deeper structures has tended since then to be unnoticed or even denied.

The issue of translations from Arab doctors is always a frustrating one, because as historians of medieval medicine always point out, Arabic terms themselves are not necessarily exact. Arabic terms for 'clitoris' are vague and uncertain. Nevertheless, the notion of a male clitoris buried in the erectile tissue of the phallus flabbergasts us, while that of a derivative 'penis' buried in the confusing vortex of the Gate of Jewels seems subconsciously plausible. However, beyond these contests of anatomical truths it seems that the splicing of the biological unit known as *Man* perpetuates itself in realms far removed from and indifferent to the theatre of reason. The androgyne fascinates because he recalls in a grotesque and theatrical way the wisdom of the anatomist. But inserted into our own routines, he irritates as much as he insults. We would, like the annoyed Olympian, much prefer to treat him as a sorb apple, take out the celestial kitchen knife, and slice him squarely down the middle.

Unfailingly aware of this scandalous fact, the androgyne himself is a melancholy animal. He/she knows perfectly well, on the other hand, that, faced with a death which has no sex, the arbitrary and ephemeral forms of the sexes melt into each other for ever.

That pessimism directed at the androgyne is as visible in the androgyne himself as in those who are suspicious of him is nowhere shown more clearly than in the journal kept by a tragic hermaphrodite in nineteenth-century France.

In Paris, in February 1868, the corpse of a young railway worker named Abel Barbin was found in a modest room on the fifth floor of a boarding house on the rue de l'Ecole de Médecine. He had committed suicide by carbonic asphyxiation and had not neglected to leave on the room's only table a letter in which it was explained that he had killed himself in order to escape from the 'sufferings' which were overwhelming him. Regnier, the *médecin de l'état civil* who recovered the letter, decided that this suffering might be due not to emotional disappointment but to raging syphilis. He therefore undertook a meticulous examination of the deceased's genital organs. What he saw astounded him, for Abel, alias Camille Barbin, was one of the most medically eccentric sexual specimens of his century, a perfectly formed hermaphrodite who had been born thirty-three years earlier as a girl.

On 18 July 1860, the *Echo Rochelais* of La Rochelle entered a paragraph on the extraordinary Abel Barbin. It noted:

> A young girl, a schoolteacher as remarkable for the elevated sentiments of her heart as for her solid education, had lived, pious and modest, up to this day in total ignorance of herself – which is to say, in the belief of being that which she appeared to be in the opinion of everyone who surrounded her. However, there were, for experienced observers, organic particularities which had astonished them, then raised doubts, and after doubt enlightenment; but the Christian education which the girl had received was the innocent blindfold which concealed from her the truth.
>
> Finally, quite recently, an accidental circumstance has occurred which has sown doubt in her mind; an appeal to science has been made, and an error of sex has been recognized. The young girl was quite simply a young man.

The *singulière métamorphose* of Barbin the girl into Barbin the boy was far from being an isolated case. What singled it out was that Abel 'himself' or Camille 'herself' wrote a confession in which she described from the inside the transformation from female to male.

Up to the moment in history in which she found herself, the hermaphrodite had been embodied only in a technical language of dissection, occasionally tinged with revulsion, amazement or pity. No one could imagine what the inner life of a hermaphrodite could be like, what its vocabulary would be, what its emotional inflexions could possibly be, for it was granted that no part of the individual is more profoundly and irremediably sexed than this secret life of the feelings which flows under and around their physiological landmarks. The genitals were directly wired up with it, so that whereas women and men had identifiable forms of secrecy appropriate to them – a whole lexicon appropriate to their sex – the inner world of the hermaphrodite was beyond the imaginable. Simply by existing, he/she brought forth a bewildering confusion.

Barbin's case was no different from other manifestations of the androgyne. By the mid-nineteenth century a considerable instrument of taxonomy was available to doctors, and Barbin's case was entered into the files of several of them. The most prominent was the article written by E. Goujon in the *Journal de l'anatomie et la physiologie de l'homme* (1869) under the title 'Etude d'un cas d'hermaphrodite imparfait chez l'homme'.

Goujon tells his reader that he and one Dr Duplomb begged Regnier to let them bag poor Barbin's amazing genital arrangements by letting them have the corpse for autopsy. One can imagine their intense excitement at the thought of preserving this staggering mélange of vagina and penis for the greater good of science. They obtained the necessary permission and made off with the incredible organs. Goujon then notes that it was now possible, with the multiplication of various forms of record, to trace the development of an important abnormality virtually from birth to death. He cites the memoirs as providing a fund of medically relevant details which can flesh out the case history.

The doctor agrees with the modification of the birth certificate – changing it from male to female – on the grounds that Barbin was a man with secondary female characteristics. However, he also notes that Barbin could make love either as a man or as a woman. At night, his sheets would be stained with effusions of seminal fluid. He could both ejaculate and receive. He was attracted towards women but was sterile. He was endowed with *un pénis imperforé susceptible d'érection*, but this mysteriously ambiguous organ was rather *un clitoris volumineux* than a penis proper.

Barbin's ejaculations were achieved by an ingenious system. The penis being without opening or duct, nothing could issue from it. The 'vagina', however, a curious cul-de-sac, had annexed to it two small conduits serving as sperm–emitters.

Goujon then describes the suicide's room: the bed with the corpse lying face down, partly dressed, the blue complexion, the ejaculation of black, frothed blood from the mouth, the thinly spread beard, the slightly hirsute and bossed nipples. The knees, he notes, are not at all inclined towards each other.

There follow detailed descriptions of internal and external organs which make reference to the medico-legal documentation accumulated for the tribunal, which had reversed the sexual identity marked on the birth certificate. The penis is carefully measured and its morphology described: five centimetres long and two and a half centimetres in diameter in a state of flaccidity. It is the size of many a clitoris.

To turn from this body of medical literature, with its talk of *vices de conformations* and its constant reference to 'these poor wretches', to the text of Barbin herself (for they deal with a period of her life when she was a woman) is to pass from an obtuse language of measurement to an older language altogether, that of the confession.

This is the first sentence: 'I am twenty-five years old and, although still young, I am approaching without doubt the final and fatal term of my existence.'

This pessimism is not inflicted by any disease or physiological disorder. Nor is it the result of a calamitous accident or the scheming of belligerent persecutors. It is a pessimism born from the condition of hermaphroditism itself.

Barbin was confined at the age of seven in

an orphanage and later transferred to a convent where, as a little girl, she received a strict and rigorous religious education. On the day of her first Communion a change occurred in her which she could not identify. Borrowing literary convention, she creates a detailed scene in which an acutely developed sense of doom emerges in the course of this momentous public ceremony:

> The atmosphere, until then tepid and perfumed, suddenly became crushingly hot. Huge black clouds scudded across the horizon presaging one of those burning storms common to this high climate. Large drops of rain soon came to confirm it, and when the procession went into the chapel, sinister flashes were already lighting up the horizon.
>
> Despite myself, my heart contracted. Was this an omen of the sombre and menacing future which was awaiting me? And was I doomed to see it appear as I put my foot on this fragile skiff that we call the world? . . . A strange malaise had overwhelmed me.

What exactly is this malaise?

In her memoirs, Camille retells her romantic 'lesbian' affairs with fellow pensioners. One after another, the pattern reveals itself: Lea, Sara, Clotilde, Thecla. The young hermaphrodite, burning with love, runs at night to their beds to kiss them or to lay an ivory cross around their necks, and is then humiliatingly intercepted by the nun on night duty.

The memoirs quickly turn into a narrative in which the determining events are those of erotic self-forgetting. Outside events, landscapes and objects simply do not exist. They are reduced to coded letters.

Arriving in her late teens at a new school, she is introduced to her class:

On all these young faces I read joy, contentment, and I remained sad, terrified! Something instinctive in me revealed itself, seeming to forbid me to enter this sanctuary of virginity. A sentiment which is powerful in me, love of study, was now diverted by the bizarre perplexity which had overwhelmed all my being.

In a few paragraphs, the critical moment of self-transformation arrives, a moment, that is, in which she feels control over her own sexual nature slipping out of her grasp and gravitating in a direction which she cannot alter.

Getting up in the morning, above all, was a torment to me . . . At that age when all the graces of a woman are developing, I had neither that full abandon nor that roundness of limb which reveals youth in all its glory. My colour, of an unhealthy paleness, denoted a state of perpetual suffering. My features had a certain hardness which one could scarcely fail to notice. A light film of hair which grew every day covered my upper lip and a part of my cheeks. You can understand how this particularly attracted jokes which I desperately tried to avoid by making frequent use of a pair of scissors by way of a razor. I merely succeeded, however, as it was doomed to be, in making it thicker still and rendering it yet more visible.

All of this was striking, and I saw it myself every day. I must say, however, that I was generally loved by my teachers and my friends and that I returned their feeling, though in a timid way. I was born for love. All the faculties of my soul impelled me in that direction; under the appearance of coldness, and almost indifference, I had a heart of fire.

In another place, she sets out the condition for her confession: 'I have to speak of things which, for many, will be nothing but incredible absurdities; for they exceed, in fact, the limits of the possible.'

From then on, she strives to make this confession. Since she feels within herself a catastrophic wound, her instinct is to heal by the act of auricular confession. For *exhomologesis*, the technical term for confession, means a 'coming to agreement with others'.

'My project was to open myself up to a confession with complete frankness and to wait for his interruption. One can imagine the astonishment, the stupefaction which my strange confession caused him!' (He later advised her to retire to a religious order and avoid public transformation into a male.)

Both as Abel and as Camille, Barbin felt a deep imperative within her to confess. To confess, that is, not just to a state of affairs, but to a *fault*. Her internal fissure has all the terrible liveliness of a disease. And her confession was nourished by the pessimism which always penetrates the androgyne as soon as he/she is aware of himself. Deprived of the natural and normal bisexuality imputed by medieval folk-lore to the hyena, the hare and the weasel, he cannot find a resting place. He has to choose one sex or the other. For, as we have seen, the male *cannot* be feminized, and the female *cannot* be masculinized. The two must always be cheese and chalk.

Conclusion

These, then, are the eight principal inventions of sexual pessimism. From the Virgin to the Androgyne, they span two and a half thousand years. Yet the reader of their histories is bound to wonder if they still exist, whether they have not been effectively buried in a remote past as strange to us as the antics in an aquarium filled with exotic fighting fish. For it is obvious that we have left sexual pessimism far behind in the Dark Ages, and that its lugubrious story is little more than a lurid melodrama from an unimaginable age.

The twentieth century prides itself on its rupture with the past. And in no respect does it consider this rupture more irremediable, and more beneficial, than in that of sexual love. Yet what it has in common with the past is its assumption that love is the key to salvation. It is just that the pessimism of Catholicism has been replaced by the equally obsessive optimism of our own Schoolmen. Psychoanalysis, which brought so much of this optimism into being, was not itself of a sunny disposition, nor in the least inclined to believe in sexual free will. But it did continue the insistence that salvation lay in the therapeutic exploration of sexuality, thus giving the latter an unchallengeable charisma. We have seen that, surprisingly, medieval theology also made sex the centre of its view of the world. All that has changed is the language.

If we have arrived at some understanding of the term *sexual pessimism*, what is there to say about its healthy sister, *sexual optimism*? The latter has its roots in secular radicalism and shares the general optimism of that radicalism as it emerged in the last half of the nineteenth century. In the sentimental songs of the Commune, for example, we find endless refrains about the 'red sun of science' and the 'dawn on the horizon'. Both leftist utopianism and anarchist reverie were based on visions of ideal sexual love. In the untroubled, normal society, this love would flow freely and spontaneously. The sexual and mental sicknesses of the bourgeoisie would be made obsolete.

In more senses than one, communism was Eden-orientated, and its early view of sex was that of a spontaneous innocence such as one might have imagined occurring in Eden without a Fall. The atheist, of course, doesn't believe in a Fall caused by sex; he believes in a Fall caused by exploitation of man by man. And so his view of Eden is not touched by sexual pessimism. There is no sin: there is only social vice.

When social vices come to embrace sexual love, as in prostitution, the radical sees only the perversion of a natural desire by social conditions. Underneath, he sees that desire as a kind of stream which can one day be restored to its natural, unpolluted state. And it was only the smallest of leaps for radical psychologists to assert that the resurrection of this sullied stream, the resurrection of *instinct*, would lead to the perfect society.

When psychoanalysis and political radicalism met in the shape of someone like Reich, all these assumptions came together in an explosive, not to say farcical, mix. But in the first communist society, too, this neutral and almost medical vision of passion exploded out of the realm of theory and – briefly – into the world of action. In Moscow in 1922 it would have been possible to stumble across crowds of naked men and women demonstrating in the streets, shouting, 'Love! Love! Down with shame! Down with shame!' True, some of the women were 'accidentally' raped on the way home, but by and large the state approved of them. Did it not itself run Free Love bureaux for a few years? The town of Vladimir even put out a Free Love decree aimed at what it called the 'socialization of women'. It makes astounding reading:

From the age of eighteen every young girl is declared state property.

Every young girl who has reached the age of eighteen and who is not married is obliged,

222

under pain of prosecution and severe punishment, to be registered at a bureau of free love.

Men likewise have the right to choose a young girl who has reached the age of eighteen if they are in possession of a certificate confirming that they belong to the proletariat . . . In the interests of the state men have the right to choose women registered at the bureau even without the assent of the latter. The children who are the fruit of this type of cohabitation become the property of the Revolution.

Between 1917 and 1923 the spirit of 'free, biological love' roamed the Soviet land, and it created a sexual culture which happily compared copulation to the drinking of a glass of water: an act of love without, as the poets put it, the cherry blossoms. The novelist Lev Gumilevsky, in his novel *Dog Lane* of 1927, has his hero confess: 'It's quite natural: I need a woman, so I turn to you, quite simply and frankly, as a friend . . . If I told you that I was hungry and that I had to go off to work, as a friend, you would willingly share a piece of bread with me, wouldn't you?' And the famous communist ideologue Alexandra Kollontai piped up to bury the green-eyed monster jealousy: 'We are banishing the notion of property from the life of the emotions.'

The so-called experiments of the 1960s pale into insignificance when put beside the chaos of the 1920s, which of course invented most of their intellectual infrastructure. There were countless projects dreamed up by fervent committees to facilitate the 'natural' sex lives of the citizens, from the installation of public rooms attached to lavatories for intercourse to the above-mentioned free-love bureaux. Psychoanalysis boomed; the abortion rate quadrupled, as did the rate of pubescent sex. And as in Nazi Germany later, schoolchildren began to form their own pornography circles.

Even late in the communist period the dextrous national manufacturing sector was devoted to the production of sex aids. In 1972 the Committee of Inventions of the Council of Ministers patented a machine (patent no. 329698) 'designed to intensify women's sexual excitement'. As the Soviet doctor Mikhail Stern put it: 'The device when in motion creates, I would imagine, a sense of perplexity in the woman, and in the man a paralysing fear of losing his penis. Nevertheless the directions for use specify that the woman should keep the apparatus switched on until the *awakening of erotic feeling*. Then, the patent tells us, *the sexual act follows as usual*.'

The de-romanticizing of sex was always seen as a stripping away of the sexual pessimism which had clung to it for centuries. And yet it is curious to see how quickly the utopia turned into a nightmare. For in order to make one's desire flow freely, one first had to be coerced into a certain shape. One had to be straightened out. And there was an even more chilling consequence of this reduction of passion: sex was reduced to breeding.

Both Nazism and communism hated the bourgeois gentrifying of erotic love. When the SS paper *Das schwarze Korps* declared that it was intent upon restoring the primeval sexuality of German women, it meant that it intended to both unleash her promiscuity and tame it with reproduction. The communist state did almost exactly the same thing. The SS writers declared: 'Woman is sacred to us in her naturally predestined role, and every man has reverence for her vocation. She is the guardian of the German race, and pure by nature. She is not the servant of the German male but his comrade and companion in life.'

'Natural sexual instincts' were continually extolled by certain Nazi ideologues, and adolescent girls in the BdM movement were tacitly encouraged to be promiscuous in order to break down the Christian barriers to fertile copulation. The Nazis needed children and they needed to whip up their people's sexual drives to get them; but at the same time, like the communists, a fear of racial contamination and social disorder led them to repress those drives. Both these two ideologies revelled in the ecstatic experience of huge crowds. In Germany in particular the orgiastic nature of Nazi ceremonies was striking – the French ambassador François-Poncet described Nuremberg as 'a city devoted to revelry and madness, a city of convulsionaries'. Hans Bleuel, in his classic study of Nazi sexual mores, called the Nazi state *convulsionary*. It glorified pagan lust, pre-Christian fertility and Earth symbolism. The problem was that it had to impose this upon a German population steeped in contrary values, the values of Christian restraint, chastity and modesty. The two were incompatible and the resulting miscegenation catastrophic. And in a slightly different way, the communist state became embattled in the same contradiction.

Is this why the *sexual optimism* of these radical states ended up petrifying in a kind of mechanical, artificial puritanism lost in the uncontrollable promiscuity which it had itself created? Bleuel shows us that the German state began to disintegrate in the middle war years under a tide of juvenile promiscuity and crime and riotous sexual disorder: what he calls a sexual revolt by the masses. Mikhail Stern, in like manner, describes the sexual abandon underlying the Soviet state, with its copulations between total strangers on public transport and its sexual tortures in the Gulag.* What in fact had happened was that the sexually optimistic state, having dispensed with all Christian restrictions, had simply gone on to try and use sex as a means of control, much in the way that their Catholic forebears had done. And it did this because, by stripping away all the pessimistic Christian baggage which tended to glorify passion and make it an intimate and tragic event, it had rendered sexual love *instrumental*. And because it was now trivial, simply a means of population increase, it became a weapon like any other. A glass of water – or a sword.

As far as the Nazis were concerned, their muddled worship of biology threw them into an identity crisis, for a society cannot simply decapitate its own past. The fascist state tried to uphold rigorous sexual and civic order based on ancient prejudices while simultaneously subverting the notion of degeneracy upon which that order had always rested in the past. In other words, instead of explaining degeneracy by means of sexual pessimism, it explained it by means of *racial pessimism*. And even if these two things crossed paths, they were not quite the same thing.

Both totalitarian states set out with almost quaint naivety to engineer souls in accordance with the 'glass of water' ethic. In the Soviet Union, prostitutes were sent to camps called *prophylactoria* to

---

* The doctor corroborates with an array of cases dealing with public transport *delicti*: 'It is for this reason that public transport constitutes a magnet, as though it were a place of pleasure and debauchery. In 1967 a 36-year-old painter came to see me and implored me to save her from "madness". She thought she was losing her mind because she was always seized by an irresistible sexual desire when in trams. It was so powerful that she was incapable of controlling it and felt ready to throw herself at men, often achieving orgasm without any other stimulation. At the same time, more often than not, she felt no desire in bed. Her visits to my surgery yielded only slight results. The patient had to give up travelling public transport. I eventually sent her to a psychiatrist colleague.'

have themselves readjusted, while in the Third Reich, state-run brothels collected semen from unwitting 'donors' in the pursuit of a plasma substitute. What Bleuel calls the 'copulatory state' in both societies grew to enormous dimensions. The Nazis set up *Lebensborn*, or Founts of Life, maternity homes for SS wives (the SS journalist Günter d'Alquen explained that they provided an opportunity for 'pre and extra-conjugal mothers of good stock to give birth under relaxing conditions') in order to harness the illegitimate children of SS indiscretions. Indeed, the Nazi state actively encouraged illegitimate children and was probably the only European state aggressively to heap public honour upon single-parent families during the war. Illegitimate children were given automatic state maintenance and state-paid guardians. Christian shame was swept under the carpet in order to let biology have its way.

Thus, whereas the Catholic Church had branded homosexuality a sin for essentially Gnostic reasons, the Nazis condemned it simply because it wasted sperm, whatever the fanaticisms of homophobe SS chiefs like Heidrich. Homosexuals in the camps were rarely tortured as they had been at the behest of the theologians, for whereas the latter wanted to purify the homosexual's soul, the former simply wanted his semen. Similarly, when the Church ordered mutilations of the flesh, it had its mystic reasons; but the Nazi policy of castrating sex offenders was an act of engineering and nothing else. The Reich Bureau of Statistics figures show that they were castrating two hundred rapists a year right up until 1945. And yet because a worship of nature and biology dehumanizes the citizen by rendering his personal passions null, a new kind of pessimism began to emerge, one that grafted itself on to the trunk of the old. The old monster gave itself new teeth.

We can see this in one unpleasant example. The Soviet exile Armand Maloumian, a former camp inmate of the 1930s, has left a disturbing account of the sexual codes used informally in the Soviet Gulag as a means of maintaining order.

Forced breeding was practised routinely in the Gulag, just as in Germany. But even worse than forced breeding was the hierarchy used to keep the male camps orderly. There, homosexual rape was used to destroy the stubborn, and in a strange and unique way.

The stubborn inmate was raped by certain homosexually active inmates and then, against his will, labelled a 'pederast'. What this did was to destroy his social status. He became an untouchable. If another convict so much as sat next to him, he too would become an *opustivshiesya*, a 'degraded'. His disease could be handed on even by the simple exchange of a cigarette.

On one occasion, Maloumian writes, at a camp near Kharkov, a delivery of anchovies caused a riot among the prisoners, because the untouchables, pushing and kicking their way to the front of the queue, succeeded in touching the fish before anyone else. Why was there a riot? Because no one else dared eat them.

Of course, homosexual coercion is an ancient tradition in prisons. But during the Stalinist period this coercion began to take the form of a codified violence which had for its intention the utter destruction of the individual's centre of gravity – a centre of gravity which Christianity had created but which the cult of biology could never for a second recognize. The prisoner started out as a sexual being with the usual attachments, perhaps some sediment of bourgeois erotic sentiment, and was then gradually humiliated and emptied until he became either a sexual gangster himself or an untouchable. In other words, he became an asexual ghost. Yet over this vast area of degradation and suffering, the state wove its predictable disguise, denying not only the use of sex as an instrument of terror, but the very existence of the homosexual form that terror had taken. Wasn't sexual love the glass of water you drank in order to increase the number of citizens? Wasn't the self, with its seething pessimism, as much an illusion as the supposed existence of Sapphics? And even as late as the 1980s the Soviet Medical Encyclopedia gave no definition of lesbian love: it merely gave the geographical location of the fabled isle of Lesbos.

The radical juggernaut did not limit itself to these grotesque aberrations, with their police dogs, barbed wire and bugged brothels. It found other forms – more iconoclastic, more agreeable. But though Wilhelm Reich, for one, lambasted the communists who had nurtured him, and reviled the Nazis as 'haters of orgasms', the basic idea common to all these revolts against Industrial Man and the Christian self remained the same. Nature was supreme; instinct was pure; sex was energy. And Life, always with a capital letter, called the tune.

As the Eden myth was given this new twist and the Noble Savage made his comeback (*Germania* delighted the Nazis as much as it had Montaigne and Rousseau), sexual pessimism entered its most curious phase yet. Just as the Schoolmen had sometimes conceived of sexual urges as a manifestation of demonic power, so Reich the erratic prophet of sexual liberation conceived of them as Orgone, that odd substance which hangs like an invisible radiation in the atmosphere. But whereas the holy eremites thought they were being persecuted by devils for telling the truth, Reich thought he was being hunted down by the US Federal Food and Drugs Administration – the problem being, *he was*.

Reich's conspiracy theory did, however, come in the end to resemble those of the demented ascetics of the deserts. Flying saucers were swooping down to prevent him from spreading his Word: didn't his Orgone Institute, buried in the woods, have orgone flak guns mounted on its roofs to shoot them down? On 10 March 1956, while driving down a lonely country road, the great psychologist was struck by a brilliant intuition: 'Are not men from outer space already living on the planet Earth? Am I really a spaceman?'

Reich thought of these extra-terrestrial supermen as formidable and tireless lovers. They were stuffed with Orgone. They had discovered the cosmic power of sexual love. The strange energy which rushed through the human body when it is making love – and which makes lovers glow blue in the dark when seen from outer space – coursed through their veins as it should through ours. Why, if we allowed ourselves to flow with Orgone by having unlimited sex, we would cease even dying of cancer!

We may think Reich quite comic, but his cosmology was more subtle and serious than Orgone-talk would lead one to believe, and vastly more influential. He is virtually the only post-war Western writer to have had his books burned by the state: on 10 August 1956, on the corner of Hudson and Ganzevoort Street in New York City, officials of the Food and Drug Administration burnt all known copies of *People in Trouble* and *Ether, God and the Devil: Cosmic Superimposition* in the public incinerator. The author survived them only by a matter of months, dying in the Federal Penitentiary at Lewisburg, Pennsylvania, in 1957. His wife liked to compare him, as in all modesty he did himself, to that other martyr who died on Golgotha. The authorities said he was mad as a hatter.

A Yugoslav film, *Mysteries of the Organism*, shows us Reich in his youth participating in some of the early propaganda films of the International Institute of Sexual Economy, in which the alarming *orgasmatherapy* is announced as the programme of *Sex-Pol* 'as taught by the revolutionary doctor and communist Wilhelm Reich'. There is Reich cavorting in a field with an accordion singing 'Beloved Communist Party, to me you are like fragrant flowers', just before a sombre voice intones: 'In our sick society everyone is sick. The human being averages 4,000 orgasms in a lifetime. Do not turn off this pulsating motor of joy and life force.' The voice goes on: 'The biological charge and discharge produced by the genital embrace causes the orgasmic reflex, supremely pleasurable muscular contractions. Subjection to social disciplines may cause gastric ulcers, respiratory, coronary and vascular diseases. Comrade lovers, for your health's sake: fuck freely.'

The 'harmonious, self-regulating workers' society' was intended to spring from this gay advice, and Reich could never forgive Lenin for being a puritan who could hardly bring himself to touch his platonic lover Inessa Armand. Reich believed that love-making would cure the following malaises:

1 industrial smog
2 infertile deserts
3 coronary thrombosis

4 inner-city crime
5 leukaemia.

He invented the notion of a sexual 'liberation', which was really the triumph of sexual love as *therapy* – but a therapy which went far beyond the pathologies of the individual.

Reich's utopianism, however, is very ancient. We have already seen it appear, again and again. The sexually liberated New Man is little more than an updated Noble Savage, an Eden-dweller – with the difference that his health is manifested in his lack of restraint, his enlightened promiscuity.

Throughout the *Mysteries of the Organism* film, in fact, we see group therapy sessions in the United States organized by Reich's disciples. People jump up and down on other people's stomachs, gnashing their teeth; couples scream at each other; roomfuls of naked bodies twist and writhe with hideous moans like the occupants of one of Dante's *bolgias*. And then we see that they are ordinary people, Mr and Mrs Jones, the local bank manager. Except that now they are writhing primitive animals screaming out their frustrations. And they have come there *to be made healthy*.

Looking at these dubiously liberated hairy animals writhing on their gym floors, one is struck by an unpleasant doubt. Are these grotesque 'patients' any better off than the penitents of the Middle Ages? Does their putative sexual health make them any less repulsive?

Reich's notion of liberation was naive but charmingly subversive. But in the end it seems utterly non-sexual. It is, after all, the submission of people to ideology, in this case a supposedly progressive one. *Mysteries of the Organism* shows us where Reich's new man ends up – on the one hand, in the communist state (as a frigid champion athlete), and on the other in the post-1960s West (as an equally frigid sybarite). The erotic, as a quality, is completely absent. And the reason for this is equally disturbing: it is that our sense of the erotic is indissolubly tied up with sexual pessimism. When we become sexual optimists, drinkers of that 'glass of water', guilt-free Reichian stallions, healthy orgasmatherapists, we turn into those drab sexual aphids so lyrically dreamed of by Gregory of Nyssa sixteen centuries ago.

What is missing from Reich's world is that elaborate code of passion which Western culture confers upon its children. This 'passion' is the fruit of the pessimistic tradition, as has already been suggested, for at the heart of the Christian–Gnostic view of the world is the belief that the soul is an inner reflection of an exterior satanic realm which it cannot control. We see this most brilliantly thought out in the Gnostic theologian Marcion of Sinope, who lived at Pontus in the second century AD and who was the butt of a Catholic hate campaign led by Tertullian, whose *Anti-Marcion* is one of the most savage of all early theological polemics.

Passion, says Marcion, lies at the heart of the human sense of self. It is what gives us our sense of authenticity. He goes on to explain that reproduction, and not sexuality, is the principal conspiracy of the demons to create more enslaved souls. He calls the world of reproduction a *hylic gulag* in which man is trapped by the force of sex.

But Marcion was also a Christian – the only great Gnostic-Christian theologian to think through the two traditions simultaneously. Hence he could not abandon the notion of a God who, though absent, involuntarily redeems his creations, even if they look like distant bacilli seen through a microscope. Yet the demonic cosmos created by Evil is reproduced in the human individual, so that the latter's inwardness is the natural scene for demonic activity. And this inner life created by an outer order is what creates 'passion' in the human individual. Sexual desire becomes the reflection of a world from which God is absent.

There is a terrifying intuition in this delicate thread of thought. We do indeed now see the world as deprived of God. And we see his dubious creation in exactly the same way as the Gnostics did. That is why their cosmology seems so modern to us. The Gnostics smelled emptiness, and they construed their notion of passion from it. Man, they said, fills his emptiness with the dreams of passion. He fills himself, as they said, with *noise*.

From this the Middle Ages derived its notion of *amor heroica*, or Heroic Love, overwhelming sexual passion which was treated as an actual disease and had all the characteristics of one: the vital spirits were thought to enter the median ventricle of the brain and could actually cause death. From this medical conception of wild love we derive the word *passio*, from the Greek *pathein*, to suffer, which also gives us 'pathology'. This word was intended simply to describe a sickness.

Medieval doctors prescribed many treatments for this strange condition of the soul, including a protracted gazing at soiled sheets. But the mystic origin ascribed to this suffering defeated them. Mere rationalism is always defenceless against the myths of passion. The latter, in any case, could not help but be glorified for its own sake, whatever its demonic origin. It made sexual love into a destructive, dangerous adventure, a disequilibrium, but also into something sacred. A sacred suffering. The lover had a Passion, we could say, directly comparable to that of Christ.

Sexual pessimism, therefore, produces not one result, but two. It destroys pleasure, but glorifies it inadvertently. It represses but cultivates passion. It scorns but exacerbates desire. It humiliates love, but then deepens it. It attempts to exterminate temptation, but succeeds only in intensifying its glamour. Trying with all its might to lift sexual love out of the human mind, it succeeds merely in making it more elaborate, more tortuous and more developed. And once its complex legacy is annulled, an eerie silence falls.

Bibliography

Andreski, Stanislav: *Syphilis, Puritanism and Witch-hunts: Historical Explanations in the Light of Medicine and Psychoanalysis with a Forecast about Aids* (Basingstoke, 1989)

Arama, Maurice: *Le Maroc de Delacroix* (Paris, 1987)

Aries, Philippe and Béjin, André, ed.: *Western Sexuality: Practice and Precept in Past and Present Times*, trans. A. Forster (Oxford, 1985)

Barbin, Abel (Adelaide Herculine): *Herculine Barbin: The Recently Discovered Memoirs of a Nineteenth-Century French Hermaphrodite* (Brighton, 1980)

Bleuel, Hans Peter: *Sex and Society in Nazi Germany*, ed. Heinrich Frankel; trans. J. Maxwell Brownjohn (Philadelphia, 1973)

Chatwin, Bruce: *The Songlines* (London, 1987)

Cleugh, James: *The Marquis and the Chevalier: A Study in the Psychology of Sex as Illustrated by the Lives and Personalities of the Marquis de Sade, 1740–1814, and the Chevalier von Sacher-Masoch, 1836–1905* (New York, 1952)

Cohn, Norman Rufus Colin: *Europe's Inner Demons: An Enquiry Inspired by the Great Witch-hunt* (London, 1975)

The Panarion of Epiphanius of Salamis, Book I, trans. Frank Williams (New York, 1987)

Flaubert, Gustave: *Letters*, ed. and trans. F. Steegmuller (Cambridge, MA, 1980–82)

——: *Flaubert in Egypt: A Sensibility on Tour*, ed. and trans. F. Steegmuller (London, 1972)

Foerster, Werner: *Gnosis: A Selection of Gnostic Texts*, ed. R. McLachlan Wilson (Oxford, 1974)

Gilman, Sander L.: *Jewish Self-hatred: Anti-Semitism and the Hidden Language of the Jews* (Baltimore, 1986)

Gonzalez–Crussi, F.: *On the Nature of Things Erotic* (San Diego, 1988)

The Gnostic Scriptures, trans. Bentley Layton (New York, 1987)

Grmek, Mirko and Coury, Charles: *La médecine de l'Amérique pré-colombienne* (Paris, 1969)

Guerra, Francisco: *The Pre-Columbian Mind: A Study into the Aberrant Nature of Sexual Drives, Drugs Affecting Behaviour and the Attitude towards Life and Death, with a Survey of Psychotherapy in Pre-Columbian America* (London, 1971)

Hedrick, Charles W.: *The Apocalypse of Adam: A Literary and Source Analysis* (Chico, CA, 1980)

Hedrick, Charles W. and Hodgson, Robert, Jr, ed.: *Nag Hammadi, Gnosticism and Early Christianity* (Peabody, MA, 1986)

Heine, Heinrich: *Religion and Philosophy in Germany: A Fragment*, trans. J. Snodgrass (Albany, NY, 1986)

Honegger, Claudia, ed.: *Die Hexen der Neuzeit: Studien zur Sozialgeschichte e. kulturellen Deutungsmusters* (Frankfurt am Main, 1979)

Institoris, Henricus, *Malleus maleficarum*, trans. M. Summers (London, 1971)

Irenaeus, Bishop of Lyons: *Against Heresies*, trans. John Keble (Oxford, 1872)

Jacquart, Danielle and Thomasset, Claude: *Sexualité et savoir médical au Moyen Age* (Paris, 1985)

John Chrysostom: *Against Remarriage*, trans. S. Rieger Shore (Lewiston, NY, 1983)

Jonas, Hans: *Zwischen Nichts und Ewigkeit: Drei Aufsatze zur Lehre vom Menschen*

Khan, Mazharul Haq: *Purdah and Polygamy: A Study in the Social Pathology of the Muslim Society* (Peshawar, 1972)

Lea, Henry Charles: *Materials Toward a History of Witchcraft* (New York, 1939)

Loti, Pierre: *Voyages, 1872–1913*, ed. C. Martin (Paris, 1991)

Mackay, Dorothy: *The Double Invitation to the Legend of Don Juan* (London, 1943)

Maloumian, Armand: *Les fils du Goulag* (Paris, 1976)

Mishima, Yukio: *The Way of the Samurai*, trans. K. N. Sparling (New York, 1977)

Nag Hammadi codices: II.6, ed. M. Scopello (Leiden, 1985) and by J.-M. Sevrin (Quebec, 1983)

BIBLIOGRAPHY

Pearson, Birger Albert: *Gnosticism, Judaism and Egyptian Christianity* (Minneapolis, 1990)

Quetel, Claude: *History of Syphilis*, trans. J. Braddock and B. Pike (London, 1990)

Rank, Otto: *The Don Juan Legend*, trans, and ed. David G. Winter (Princeton, NJ, 1975)

Ranke-Heinemann, Uta: *Eunuchs for Heaven: The Catholic Church and Sexuality*, trans. J. Brownjohn (London, 1990)

Reich, Wilhelm: *Ether, God and the Devil: Cosmic Superimposition*, trans. Therese Pol (New York, 1973)

——: *The Function of the Orgasm: Sex-Economic Problems of Biological Energy*, trans. V. R. Carfagno (New York, 1973)

Rougemont, Denis de: *L'amour et l'Occident* (Paris, 1972)

Rudolph, Kurt: *Gnosis: The Nature and History of Gnosticism*, ed. R. McLachlan Wilson (San Francisco, 1983)

Sevely, Josephine Lowndes: *Eve's Secrets: A New Perspective on Female Sexuality* (New York, 1987)

Sinistrari, Lodovico, *Demonolatry*, trans. M. Summers (London, 1927)

Sissa, Giulia: *Greek Virginity*, trans. A. Goldhammer (Cambridge, MA, 1990)

Sontag, Susan: *Illness as Metaphor* (New York, 1987)

Spector, Jack J.: *Delacroix: The Death of Sardanapalus* (New York, 1974)

Topsfield, L.T.: *Troubadours and Love* (London, 1975)

Veyne, Paul: *Did the Greeks Believe in their Myths? An Essay on the Constitutive Imagination*, trans. P. Wissing (Chicago, 1988)

Warner, Marina: *Alone of All Her Sex: The Myth and Cult of the Virgin Mary* (London, 1976)

Watanabe, Tsuneo: *Love of the Samurai: A Thousand Years of Japanese Homosexuality*, trans. D. R. Roberts (London, 1989)

Lawrence Osborne writes a column for *Newsday*, New York, and is a full-time staff writer at the *San Diego Reader*. He is the author of the novels *Ania Malina* and *The Angelic Game*, and the travelogue *Paris Dreambook*. He lives in New York.